MOVING MOUNTAINS

MOVING MOUNTAINS

Discovering Joy Through Suffering

TERRI KERN, MIKE KERN WITH TINA WENDLING

Moving Mountains: Discovering Joy Through Suffering by Mike and Terri Kern with Tina Wendling

Cover design by Donna Filman.

Scripture references used in this work are taken from the New American Bible, revised edition © 2010, 1991, 1986, 1970 Confraternity of Christian Doctrine, Inc., Washington, DC All Rights Reserved.

ISBN-13: 9781537093376
ISBN-10: 1537093371
Library of Congress Control Number: 2016918598
CreateSpace Independent Publishing Platform
North Charleston, South Carolina
Printed in the United States of America.

Available at Amazon.com and other book retailers.

For our five beautiful children
who have been,
and continue to be,
true blessings to us both

CONTENTS

Introduction

IT STARTS WITH PRAYER

**The following excerpt is taken from a letter
written by Terri Kern to her husband, Mike,
in February 2008, just two months before
her terrifying accident on April 28, 2008.
It recounts events beginning in 2006
that undoubtedly prepared her and
her family for what was to come.**

It all started with a prayer. On September 20, 2006, I prayed for my husband to be burdened for his health. I had been getting up early in the morning to have my prayer time and daily conversations with Jesus. Many times, I would just sit and listen to what God might be telling me to do. I have a spot in our piano room on the floor where I pray. In fact, the wooden cabinet I lean back on is discolored from all the mornings I've sat there. It is a constant reminder for me of the importance of daily prayer. I don't know why I hadn't taken my concerns about Mike's health to God in prayer before, but on this particular morning I did, and that prayer set off a series of events that would change my marriage, my husband, and most importantly my faith and relationship with the Lord.

Just nine days later, Mike became very ill with what we both thought was some sort of flu bug. It began with a fever and stomach pains, but after several days, it worsened to the point where he needed to go to the emergency room. A CAT scan revealed that his colon was infected (diverticulitis), and he may need surgery.

Now, I know I prayed that he would start to take his health seriously, but this wasn't exactly what I had in mind. He was miserable and in so much pain, and I was scared. I cried out to God and truly felt the comfort of His embrace, as if He was buoying me up and giving me peace so that I could be strong.

Mike was in the hospital for almost a week, although it felt like much longer. He hated being alone and was so anxious to get home. Fortunately, he averted surgery, and once home, he tried hard to adhere to the recommended diet.

We continued to go through a series of trials, all the while leaning on God. We didn't know what else to do. There was a point when I did tell Mike of my prayer that he would be burdened for his health. "Do me a favor and quit praying for me," he said with a smile.

As time went on, I was amazed at how this had changed Mike. In a completely uncharacteristic move, he actually asked me to take a walk with him one day. Previously, he liked to play tennis or basketball to exercise, but he would have never initiated a walk. I just looked up to the heavens and giggled at how creative God is and how I continue to be amazed at how a bad situation can become good -- Romans 8:28: *"God works all things for the good for those who love him and are called according to his purpose."*

Just when I thought we had come through the woods, Mike started having severe back pain that radiated down his arm and into his leg, causing him to limp. He tried acupuncture, physical therapy, cortisone shots, and even an inversion table! Nothing seemed to work, and in fact, it worsened to the point where Mike became non-functional. He could not sit down, so he stood or laid on the floor. He ate on the floor and many times slept on the floor. At work, he stood or laid on the floor as well. It pained the kids and me to see Mike suffering like this. I often found him on the floor in our bathroom, crying out in pain. He was having a hard time, and on occasion, we both got angry. This suffering, however, brought us one step closer to Christ.

On Good Friday, Mike came home in tremendous pain. He said he simply could not do this anymore. I remember looking at him with tears in my eyes, telling him that he could continue and that God would get us through this -- 1 Thessalonians 5:16-18: *"Be joyful always; pray continually; give thanks in all circumstances, for this is God's will for you in Christ Jesus."* Wow, we were supposed to be joyful? Give thanks? We didn't want to do this. I guess that is when we began to surrender and offer up this suffering to God. We quit trying to understand it, but rather began to trust His plan.

During that Good Friday service, I remember looking toward the back of the church and seeing my dear husband carrying the cross to the altar. At that moment, I not only saw this big heavy cross, but the spiritual cross that Christ bore. It was so clear – how Christ selflessly carried His cross and ours as well. Knowing Christ is with us is so very comforting; however, it doesn't lessen the pain. Mike's pain continued to worsen. He had no appetite and was losing weight. He continued to take medication and do some physical therapy, with no relief.

On May 22, 2007, after more severe stomach pain, another CAT scan revealed that Mike was again suffering from diverticulitis and needed to be hospitalized. I have never seen my husband so upset. When I arrived at the hospital, I found him in his car lying down. He looked like he was ready to stop fighting. He couldn't take much more, and the last thing he wanted to do was spend time in the hospital. After begging and pleading with his doctor, it was agreed that he could recover at home with IV antibiotics, but that meant I would have to administer them. This scared me; I was not a nurse and had no idea what to do. They explained that a nurse would come over to the house and teach me how to administer the medication through a Picc (peripherally inserted central catheter) line. I didn't want Mike to know how nervous I was, because he really did want to come home, so I simply said, "Sure, I can do that." Of course, I was thinking to myself, "Please Lord, give me the strength and energy to do this."

While Mike did get to come home, he did not look well. He had lost quite a bit of weight and his back was still causing him so much pain, and now he needed to lie in bed and receive IV antibiotics for five days. The nurse came that evening and unloaded all the supplies. She taught me how to flush the Picc line, time the drip, decide which medication to administer at which time, and many more instructions that seemed to go on and on. I kept a brave face for Mike, but the whole time, I was realizing how much I needed God.

Mike also kept a smile on his face, but I sensed that behind the smile lurked confusion, frustration, and anger. Mike continued to love the Lord and kept faith in His plan; however, he also felt defeated at times and worried about providing for our family.

We lay in bed at night with the IV dripping, praying and holding one another, often crying together. Neither one of us could imagine how or when this would end. We cried out many times to God asking for it to end. Instead, He gave us a stronger marriage, stronger faith, and true compassion. Apparently, God knows what is best for us (light bulb moment).

Once we made it over that hurdle, Mike had to make a decision about his back pain. The bulging disc that was pressing on a nerve root, causing pain throughout his entire right side, needed to be addressed once and for all, which meant surgery. Mike was hesitant, but with careful prayer, he decided it was time.

Mike hadn't been sleeping in our bed for months. He had moved into our youngest daughter's (Halley) room, which is right off our bedroom. He was up quite a bit and it was difficult to sleep with me moving around. Halley took up a permanent spot on the floor next to my bed. It was like a sleepover that never ended! Mike was more comfortable sleeping alone, although I missed him terribly in so many ways. I missed his sarcasm, his humor, and the way he was always lovin' on me, like he couldn't get enough of me. He had become withdrawn and frustrated.

I would often hear him cry out in pain during the night, and I became very frustrated because I couldn't do anything to relieve his pain. We continued to pray for His strength -- Philippians 4:13: *"You can do all things through Christ who strengthens you."*

Many times, Mike and I would both ask God what he was teaching us. We started to believe we must be slow learners. God's timing is perfect, but this is hard to remember when you are suffering or watching the man you love so dearly suffer in such pain. I wished I could have taken on some of the pain. I felt so helpless and also a bit guilty for being able to do all those things we take for granted. Not that we had much choice in the matter, but, we decided to do what Scripture tells us to do -- Psalm 27:14: *"Wait for the Lord; be strong and take heart and wait for the Lord."*

It was difficult, but I tried to maintain some normalcy for the children. They had witnessed their dad on the floor in such pain; it brought tears to their eyes. The kids had many questions, some I couldn't answer. They continued to pray for their father. God was teaching us all a good lesson about compassion and suffering. This was our opportunity to model faith and trust in God for our children, even when things are not going well. I hope Mike and I taught our children that and didn't blow this opportunity. I would hate to have to do it again.

On the Saturday before Mike's surgery, I decided to cut some tree limbs down. Mike wanted some fresh air, so he hobbled outside to see what I was doing. The trimmer slipped from my grip and landed on Mike's ankle, cutting him badly. I rushed him inside, blood gushing all over the kitchen floor. As I began pressing rags on the cuts, I completely lost it. Tears were pouring out as I kept apologizing. I made the mistake of asking him if it hurt. He looked at me and said, "Compared to what?" I told him I thought he may need stitches. He refused. I continued to cry. I had had enough. Mike looked up at me and said "Terri, it was an accident, don't let Satan in." That was all I needed to hear -- Ephesians 6:11: *"Put on the full armor of God so that you can take your stand against the devil's schemes."*

The night before surgery, when I went in to tell Mike good night and pray with him, he said he wanted to discuss some things with me. He said, with surgery, there is always a risk. Something could go wrong.... Mike likes to cover all the bases. I, however, just knew everything was going to be fine. Maybe that is why we work well together; he likes to be prepared, and I will prepare if I need to. He said, "If anything should happen to me, I want you to move on with your life. I want you to be happy, and know that I don't regret anything that has happened. I love you so much and thank God every day for you and our five beautiful children." That is how we left it. Mike needed to say it. Without arguing, I just listened and then went to bed in tears.

We awoke very early on Tuesday, June 26, 2007. We prayed together that morning, which is one of my fondest memories. We prayed that the surgery would be successful, that God would guide the surgeon's hand, and most importantly, we prayed that God would give us the strength and courage to accept whatever the outcome might be. I remember praying Colossians 3:15-*"Let the peace of Christ rule in your hearts, since as members of one body you were called to peace."* This was it.... I so wanted to have that peace actually RULE in my heart. After many hours in the waiting room, the surgeon said everything went well. He said a fragment of Mike's disc had pinned his nerve root. The surgeon indicated that Mike must have been in tremendous and constant pain. I was so thankful all had gone well and looked upward to God with a big "thank you."

When I went to see Mike after he was out of recovery, he smiled, as he always does when he doesn't want me to worry. I relayed to him that the surgery was successful. Mike looked so relieved. He said he could no longer feel the throbbing pain that had been such a part of his life for the last eight months. I brought the kids up to see him later. The kids were so excited to hear that their dad's back was better -- James 1:12: *"Blessed is the man who perseveres under trial, because when he has stood the test, he will receive the crown of life that God has promised to those who love him."*

Mike came home a couple days later and required a lot of aftercare initially. It made us both realize that one uses their back for essentially everything. He was not to bend over at all. This made getting dressed, using the bathroom, getting out of bed, reaching for things, etc. impossible to do without help.

His aftercare required him to walk around a bit. He would very slowly circle around the inside of the house. We had fun counting his "laps." Sponge baths...you think they would be kind of fun, but I think Mike and I would both agree that they are not fun when you're sick. I changed his dressing twice daily. We also found a very inventive way to wash his hair by lying on the bed. Mike kept saying to me "Sorry, Terri... in sickness and in health, huh?" I really didn't mind, and I loved caring for him.

I do remember crying one night, thanking God for His constant presence throughout this journey. I tend to be strong through the crisis, but fall apart when it is over. I hadn't cried that hard until Mike moved back into the bed. I began to realize all we had been through and would continue to go through together. This journey was not one that either one of us signed up for; however, I wouldn't have changed it for anything. Mike and I had both been changed, our marriage had changed, our priorities had changed, and most importantly, our relationship with Jesus Christ had changed.

Saint Paul speaks about rejoicing in our sufferings. I never completely understood that. How and why would someone rejoice while suffering? I understand this now. Through suffering, we are drawn closer to God. Through suffering, we become more like Christ. Through suffering, our faith is tested -- Romans 5:3-5: *"Not only so, but we also rejoice in our sufferings, because we know that suffering produces perseverance; perseverance, character; and character, hope. And hope does not disappoint us, because God has poured out his love into our hearts by the Holy Spirit, who he has given us."*

I thank God every day for my husband; I thank God for the journey he has seen us through. I am not sure how to end this because I feel like this journey is not yet over. We will continue to face trials and struggles; in fact, we still are. We are still speaking with doctors concerning Mike's colon and the diverticulitis. We are trying to gather information to decide if surgery is the best option. We continue to place our trust in the Lord, the one who is the constant through all things. I have truly been blessed with a husband who has a heart for the Lord and five beautiful children. Why did I write this? It is simple. Many times, we go through things in our lives that shape who we are. Many times, we forget the details and forget to give God the glory. We tend to get back into the normal routine of things. I do not ever want to forget this period in my life. Throughout this struggle, we saw and experienced such joy, hope, and love -- Philippians 4:19: *"And my God will meet all your needs according to his glorious riches in Christ Jesus."*

-February 2008

VOICES

This story is narrated from the voices of several different people in addition to Mike and Terri Kern: Each of their five children, Kaitlyn, Courtney, Abby, John Milton, and Halley; Terri's mother, Kay; Lynn Hillring and Coleen Weller, both friends of Terri's; Mike's basketball coaching partner, Dr. Bob Thompson, and Terri's neurosurgeon, Dr. Paul Camarata.

KAITLYN

Kaitlyn is the oldest and never lets her siblings forget it. She is fiercely independent, funny, smart, and would do anything for her family. She was almost **seventeen** at the time of the accident, and true to form, she took on the real-life role of "mom" that she had always portrayed when the kids played house. In her matter of fact manner, she saw things as they were and did what needed to be done. She grew up quickly and is now a successful teacher, a compassionate friend, and an advocate for others who are suffering.

COURTNEY

Barely **fifteen** at the time of the accident, Courtney was just finishing her freshman year of high school. She was always spiritual and continues to draw strength from her faith and her relationship with God. A natural performer, she was involved in theater and music growing up, but as a young adult, her passions have led her to travel, learn different languages, and explore new cultures. She is devoted to service and justice causes, both domestic, and international, and is currently serving with the Jesuit Volunteer Corps in Micronesia.

ABBY

Determined in all areas of her life, Abby is extremely committed to school and family, and always shows up even if it's hard. Sensitive and empathetic, she has a way of always including everyone. She is extremely witty and possesses a great sense of humor. At **thirteen**, she was inspired by the care Terri received from the nurses at the numerous hospitals she was in and the myriad of ways the nurses ministered to the entire family. Eight years later, Abby is in nursing school and devoted to the care of the whole person and the whole family.

JOHN MILTON

John Milton is the only boy and he owns it. He graciously endures his sisters, plays off Abby with even wittier jokes, and enjoys his relationship with his dad. He is strong and extremely likable, honest and direct, compassionate and dependable. He is a man of few words, but loves his family deeply. He was only **eleven** at the time of the accident and tried hard to "man up" and take care of his sisters. He's a self-proclaimed "realist" who sees the world as it is and accepts it that way.

HALLEY

Halley marches to the beat of her own drum and does not care what anyone thinks. She oozes self-confidence and lights up a room when she enters. Loving and unafraid to show it, she has a remarkably positive outlook about everything. She is thoughtful and never forgets a birthday or any sort of special occasion. Barely **six** at the time of the accident, she barely remembers life before it. Now, at fifteen, her faith in God's plan is unwavering, and she believes whole-heartedly that her mom survived for a greater purpose.

KAY

Kay is Terri's mother and an important part of this journey of faith. Leaving behind her normal routine, she and her husband, Allan, moved to Kansas City for the duration of Terri's recovery. Kay loved spending that time with her grandchildren and sees many blessings that came from this difficult experience.

LYNN

Lynn Hillring has been a close friend of Terri's since meeting almost twenty years ago when they moved in to the same neighborhood. Lynn was instrumental in helping organize carpools, meal deliveries, prayer support, and everything else necessary to keep the Kern family afloat during this time.

COLEEN

Coleen Weller, another close friend of Terri's from church, was also instrumental in organizing schedules and meals for the Kern family. Coleen was deeply moved by Terri's example of faith and prayer and credits her for her own daily prayer life and relationship with God and His angels.

DR. BOB THOMPSON

Bob Thompson coached his daughter's basketball team with Mike Kern and knew the Kern family from the Church of the Nativity in Leawood, KS. He also happens to be an ENT, so when he found out about Terri's accident, he went to the hospital to see if he could be of any help to Mike. Out of the sheer goodness of his heart, he ended up staying by Mike's side, becoming a medical advocate during a very tenuous couple of days.

DR. PAUL CAMARATA

Paul Camarata, a Kansas City neurosurgeon, just happened to attend the same church as Mike and Terri. While their children were friends, the connection between the Kerns and Camaratas was loose at best. A man of deep faith and persistent prayer, he agreed to take on Terri's case even when it seemed like all hope was lost. Paul not only treated Terri, but became her medical advocate as well, navigating the many unforeseen twists and turns as only a true professional can.

Chapter 1

THE DAY AGAINST WHICH ALL DAYS WILL BE MEASURED

"No trial has come to you but what is human. God
is faithful and will not let you be tried beyond your
strength; but with the trial he will also provide
a way out, so that you may be able to bear it."

1 Corinthians 10:13

TERRI

I shouldn't be alive. No mistake about it – I should've died on April 28, 2008. That was the day that changed everything...forever.

It started like any other day. I woke at 5:30 and quietly crept downstairs for my daily prayer time and journaling. With my cup of coffee in hand, I settled myself in my usual spot on the floor and leaned back against the cabinet the way I always did. That time with God every morning was my life-line. I had come to depend on it to start my day. Growing up in Utah with the majestic beauty of the Wasatch Mountain

Range right in my backyard, I could not help but feel the presence of God all around me. I have fond memories of my childhood; however, amid a heavily Mormon population, I sometimes struggled to feel like I was part of a Catholic community. It was refreshing when I met Mike to see how open and expressive his large family was, and it was a blessing in our marriage that our shared faith was so central to our family life. Raising five children and being married to a husband who often traveled for his job were sometimes daunting tasks – I knew I needed God's help, so that's why I started every day in conversation with Him. I knew I couldn't do it without Him.

After dropping our youngest three at school, I contemplated whether I had time in my already over-scheduled day to squeeze in a run. Deciding I did, I grabbed a jacket and some earmuffs because it was unseasonably chilly for late April. I set out, being careful to time it just right so that I would not be late to pick up Halley, our youngest, from kindergarten at 11:00.

That morning, I wasn't particularly "up" for a run, and as I got going, my mind began to wander. My family had been through so much in the last year and a half, it was still hard for me to process it all and wrap my brain around it. Mike had suffered through many months of excruciating back pain and diverticulitis – completely unrelated, but cruelly coincidental. At the time, it wreaked havoc on our family's life. Mike was completely incapacitated at times and was literally leveled by the pain. Much of my time over the last year had been dedicated to caring for him, both pre- and post-surgery. He was finally on the mend, well enough to return to work, which meant I could resume my normal routine, so I was slowly trying to get back to my daily 3-4 mile run. It felt great to be able to get out and move, but it also felt oddly selfish. That day, especially, I was thinking about how much I took for granted. After watching Mike struggle all year just to walk or sit upright without enduring grueling pain, the ability to go for a run felt like a lavish indulgence, an enormous blessing. I was feeling abundantly fortunate and so grateful to God for Mike's recovery and for all the support we had received from friends and family along the way.

I wouldn't even remember the irony of this line of thinking for many months to come, but that was my frame of mind that morning... gratitude and relief – relief that we had come through this season of suffering and were now on the other side of it and could hopefully move forward. I say "hopefully" because as eerie as it seems now, there was something nagging at me from deep within. As much as I wanted to believe we *had* come through this season of suffering, it was as if I knew that there was still more to come.

That's when it happened. I was crossing a four-lane road right at the entrance of our subdivision, heading home and to the shower, when a large SUV traveling at forty-five miles per hour careened into me, propelling me thirty-five feet through the air. I hurtled past a light pole, landing miraculously on a four-foot patch of grass. That would be the first of many miracles to come.

Thankfully, I don't have any real memory of actually being hit, which is a blessing because I don't have to relive it over and over again in my mind. According to eyewitnesses, I sat up and asked the first responder, who happened to be a pastor from a nearby church, to call 911 and my husband, Mike – I even gave him the correct number! Mike beat the ambulance to the hospital, and I do remember that once I saw him, I went immediately into "mom" mode – Who was picking Halley up from kindergarten? Courtney had CYT (Christian Youth Theater) practice that evening. John Milton had a game. Mike did a great job of soothing my worries and reassuring me that all the details would be handled.

Initially, the doctors didn't think my injuries were too terribly serious. I didn't look pretty – lots of bruises and gashes to the face and legs – but otherwise, I appeared stable, and the emergency medical team seemed to think I would be all right. No sooner had that been said, everything went black. I couldn't see anything and I couldn't feel anything. I panicked. "Am I paralyzed?" I desperately pleaded with Mike for an explanation. The doctor immediately ordered a CT scan which revealed I was throwing blood clots and having a series of strokes. While they couldn't explain exactly why this was happening, they knew it was far more serious than they first anticipated. Something was seriously wrong. The hospital I was in was a small, regional hospital that was just not equipped for a trauma like mine. I needed to be moved, and it needed to happen quickly. Coming in and out of consciousness, I heard bits and pieces, but my memory of it is sparse at best. What I do remember is that I knew I was in serious trouble. I couldn't articulate it, but I remember thinking, "This must be pretty bad!"

MIKE

Clots. Strokes. Internal bleeding. Loss of oxygen. Not equipped to treat her...

I heard the words, but I couldn't ascribe any meaning to them in my brain. They were just strings of letters and sounds floating in the air but not seeping in. *What did it all mean?*

It had only been a few short hours since the phone call. I was so immersed in the project I had been working on that morning that the ringing of my phone startled me and I hesitated to answer it. It was from a number, and then a voice, that I didn't recognize, but a voice I will never forget.

"Hello, is this Mike?"

"Yes, it is. Who's this?"

"My name is John. Your wife has been in an accident. She wanted me to call you. I think she's okay, but they're taking her to Overland Park Regional."

It was as if something unhinged inside me. I went into auto-pilot, grabbing my keys and running out the door without even thinking. The hospital was so close to my office that I actually beat the ambulance there. As I was frantically trying to get some – any – information, they wheeled Terri in. She was pretty badly banged up, but coherent and immediately went into task-manger mode when she saw me, asking all sorts of questions about school pick up and relaying to me all the details of who needed to be where for the rest of the day.

Terri was truly a supermom, handling the busy schedules of our five children in a way that made it look effortless. I was in awe of her and more in love with her now, after almost twenty years of marriage, than I was the day I proposed. She had been a trooper, moving all over the country for my job and never complaining, giving up her own career as a social worker to raise our family. She was my rock, especially during the last year and a half when I had gone through so many health problems. I had often thought during that time, that if the tables were turned, I would not have been nearly the compassionate caregiver to her that she was to me. Little did I know then how soon the tables *would* be turned, and how the words, "in sickness and in health," would test me to the core.

Initially, the doctors reported Terri to be stable, assuring me she would be all right. When the officer on the scene of Terri's accident asked to speak with me, his level of concern was unsettling. He appeared worried and wanted to know how she was doing and what the doctors were saying. The expression on his face as he listened to my answers didn't match the optimistic news I was relaying to him, and finally he explained, "Mr. Kern, you understand that your wife wasn't in her car when this happened? She was a pedestrian hit by a moving vehicle at forty-five miles per hour." I was speechless. I guess I just assumed Terri had been hit in her car, and with this new revelation, I immediately understood the look on his face and what it was conveying. He didn't even have to say it, I got the message loud and clear. He had been a police officer for a long time and had seen it all. People didn't walk away unharmed from accidents like this -- there was no way Terri was going to be all right.

So I guess it shouldn't have surprised me when Terri started saying she couldn't feel her arms or legs and that everything was black, but it *did* surprise me. Honestly, it terrified me in a way no words can express. I didn't know what to do – she was panicked, and desperate, and I was helpless. She kept asking me, "Am I paralyzed? Am I going to die? Mike, am I going to DIE?" I ran to get the doctor, and suddenly, the scene changed. It was just like what you see in the movies or on TV – the little ER room was overrun with doctors and nurses, like tiny ants scuttling in every direction. They were shouting orders and rolling in machinery while someone pushed me out the door, saying "Sir, you'll have to wait outside."

"What the hell is happening?" I kept repeating, but no one answered. I was escorted into a small waiting room just off the emergency area, the door slamming shut behind me. Silence engulfed me. I was all alone. I felt all alone – more alone than I have ever felt in my entire life. My head was throbbing, and I couldn't stop envisioning Terri's frightened face. I felt like I was being swallowed up by a giant black pit of hopelessness and despair. It felt like Satan himself was staring me down, taunting me with so many questions, so much doubt, and an unbearable fear. *Am I going to lose Terri?* The faces of my five children flashed before my eyes, and all I could think was, *How the hell am I supposed to raise FIVE kids by myself?* Terri's face flashed before my eyes – *Oh God, what is she experiencing right now? Is she afraid? Is she in pain?*

I did the only thing I know to do when I am feeling that kind of darkness and angst. I dropped to my knees in prayer. I knew there was nothing else I could do. I had absolutely no control over the outcome of this situation. I *had* to give it to God. I don't know exactly how long I was on my knees, but not that much time could've passed when I felt a hand on my shoulder. Startled, I opened my eyes and looked up to find one of my best friends, John Hillring, standing above me. "Anything I can do?" he asked.

"Pray." It was the only word I could utter, and without hesitation, John knelt beside me and we prayed together. Buoyed up by this prayer, John's encouragement, and the fact that it was about time for school to be dismissed, I knew I had to go home and tell the kids what had happened. John's wife, Lynn, had arrived by that time, so I felt comfortable leaving, knowing Terri was in good hands with our dearest friends by her side.

LYNN

Terri was an absolute blast to be around. I loved how much fun I always had being with her, but I also loved how calm, cool, and collected she was at all times. During our ten-year friendship, I had seen what a grounded, faith-filled, caring woman of prayer she really was, and I had a deep admiration and respect for her. When my husband John called to tell me she had been in an accident, even though he assured me she had not been seriously injured, I was a little panicked. *She was hit by a car! How can she not be seriously injured?* Since the depth of Terri's injuries was unknown at that point, I believed what John said – she's going to be ok – and I headed up to the hospital to see if I could help.

Terri actually looked better than I expected, although I am not sure exactly *what* I expected. She was coherent and talking with me, and at one point, she said, "I can't feel my right side."

I, of course, trying to reassure her, just kept saying, "Well honey, you were hit by a car. You're gonna be fine, you're just in shock. It's all going to be ok." I had no idea what was coming or what it really meant that she couldn't feel her right side, but I think at that point, *she* already knew that something was terribly wrong.

MIKE

How do you tell your five children that the person they have come to rely on for almost everything is laying in a hospital bed with injuries that seem to be worsening? The only answer to this question was prayer because I knew I couldn't do this without God's help. As I drove home, I prayed out loud, "Heavenly Father, please send the Holy Spirit and give me strength to convey the enormity of what has happened to our children."

Our oldest, Kaitlyn, soon to be seventeen, and Courtney, right behind her at fifteen, were the first two I saw when I pulled in to the driveway. After blurting out the news to them both, Courtney went inside. Typical of Kaitlyn's strong, mothering personality, she listened to me, let me cry on her shoulder, reminded me that God is good, and then immediately started to help me relay the information to the other children as they arrived home – first Abby, then John Milton, and finally Halley. I don't remember much of these conversations. For the most part, it was fairly matter of fact, and I admit that in retrospect, I probably did not do the best job of conveying the severity or extent of Terri's situation to our children. I don't think *I* completely understood the severity or extent of what was happening at that point, but even if I did, I know I didn't have any clue how to share this terrible news with them.

ABBY

"Oh my gosh! Dad's home!" We were all so excited. Dad was *never* home this early. In my total thirteen-year-old naiveté, I thought he must have come home to surprise us. Maybe we were going on a trip or even just to get ice cream, I didn't know. Whatever it was, I never thought, in a million years, that he was home to tell us our mom had been in a horrible accident. The worst-case scenario never even entered my mind.

Why would it? Our family had never been through anything like that before. We lived a carefree, happy life, playing outside, making forts in the living room, dressing John Milton up like a girl. Life had been good! I had no idea it could be otherwise.

It was unsettling for me to see my dad cry. Dads aren't supposed to do that. I had never seen him cry before, and although it was a little frightening, I kept talking to myself, "Well, ok, she's alive, so that's good. As long as she's alive, it's all going to be fine."

MIKE

Thinking that it was a good idea for the kids to see their mom, I loaded everyone up in the van and headed to the hospital. As we were walking toward the waiting room, the elevator doors opened, and we literally ran into Terri being wheeled off, semi-unconscious and banged up – not exactly how I had planned for the kids to see her for the first time since the accident. They all ran straight to the gurney asking their Mom how she was doing, and of course, it did not take long for the frightening reality of her condition to set in.

COURTNEY

Kaitlyn and I had just gotten home from school when my dad met us on the driveway. He quickly told us that our mom had been in a car accident, and that we needed to go to the hospital to see her. I remember not being too worried because he had seemed okay, and he hadn't said anything about her being hit while she was running. I was just learning to drive at that point, so I think I registered it as a sort of fender bender. No big deal.

Pulling in the hospital parking lot, I was in pretty good spirits – we all were. We still didn't understand the severity of the situation, but that was all about to change. As we were winding through the hospital corridors, we ran smack dab into our mom being wheeled into the elevator for tests, and we all froze. It was as if time literally stood still, and that moment will be forever forged in my memory. She was horribly bruised and she seemed delirious. She was crying, her eyes were darting everywhere, and she kept repeating, "Those are my kids. Please stop, those are my kids. I love my kids!" She was the epitome of terrified, and we could all read it very clearly on her face. As the elevator doors closed, I remember hearing my mom scream for Halley, and that is the moment I knew this was serious. We wandered around for a while after that through the hospital like little lost puppies, Kaitlyn trying to hold us all together, but we had seen what we had seen, and there was no glossing over it.

We were able to see her after they ran some tests, and by that point, she actually seemed "better." She was making sense, talking about our schedules and who needed to be where when. We were even laughing at her because she kept repeating things like, "Courtney you have acting class tonight. Don't forget." I think I was so relieved to talk to her that I didn't even question why she was repeating things or why her voice sounded funny. We all left with a strong sense that everything was going to be all right.

MIKE

After sending the kids home with close family friends, I hunkered down for a long night. My friend and CYO basketball-coaching partner, Dr. Bob Thompson, surprised me that night with a visit. He had heard about Terri's accident from his daughter, who was close friends with Abby, and out of the sheer goodness of his heart, came to check on me to see if I needed anything. What a God-send! He was such a source of comfort, information, and advocacy in those early hours that quickly stretched into days. There were no immediate answers, but Dr. Thompson stayed by me the entire time.

DR. BOB THOMPSON

I'm not sure exactly what compelled me to get involved with this situation. We weren't all that close with the Kerns, although our daughters were friends, and Mike and I coached their CYO basketball team together. We knew them from church, and even though we weren't social friends, I knew I liked them, and I knew they were a great family. When my daughter told me that Terri was in the hospital, I called Mike to make sure everything was okay, fully expecting him to tell me it was not a big deal and that she was going to be fine. That was not at all what happened.

When I spoke to Mike, he was alone in the radiology suite, unsure of what was going on. He explained everything that had occurred, starting with the initial prognosis that Terri had not sustained any serious trauma, but how things changed when she started saying she couldn't see or feel anything. I knew something was terribly wrong, and I thought about Mike being there all alone, waiting for answers and not getting any. I tried to put myself in his shoes. *How would that feel?* Mike's daughter Abby had called to ask my daughter for a ride to basketball practice, not necessarily to tell us about Terri, but after speaking with Mike, I decided basketball practice could wait. I needed to go be with him. I knew Mike was the kind of guy who would have done the same for me.

MIKE

As that first night wore on, the answers slowly started rolling in, like a wave crashing over my head. That's when they started using words like, "clots" and "strokes." Whatever they had thought initially about Terri being okay had been thrown out the window and replaced with a new and frightening diagnosis. The doctor's words were like searing flames to my flesh. We were not at a "stroke facility," so there wasn't much they could do. Terri's best chance for survival was to be moved.

Chapter 2

DECISIONS

*"Wait on the Lord, take courage; be
stouthearted, wait for the Lord!"*

PSALM 27:14

MIKE

I consider myself a decisive man, but nothing can prepare you to make the kind of life and death decisions that a crisis like this calls for. I am used to consulting with Terri on major decisions, talking things over and weighing our options. How could I navigate this without her? I had no choice – Terri had lost consciousness, so I had to go it alone, and I had to act quickly. When the doctors suggested that Terri be moved, I looked to Bob Thompson for insight. I knew he was a good man, so I readily listened to him when he advised me that we should transport Terri to a hospital in downtown Kansas City where he knew a neuro-surgeon named Paul Camarata. Bob was convinced that he would be the best doctor for Terri. If only it were that easy.

As it turned out, that facility, St. Luke's, was not available because Dr. Camarata and his team were attending a conference in Chicago. *So now what?* Next decision. That option was off the table, so again with Bob's counsel, I decided to have Terri taken to a different Kansas City hospital, larger than the one she was currently in and hopefully better equipped to treat her. Although it was only fifteen miles away, that twenty-minute drive was a lonely one that night. I can't describe the eerie feeling of following the ambulance that is carrying your wife, grappling with the fear that she may not survive, and staring in the face of the cold hard truth that no one knows exactly what is happening to her or why.

LYNN

Mike asked me to stay with the kids that first night. Once I got everyone settled in bed, I took a long, deep breath, and began to pray. I felt very uneasy about the situation, like a giant question mark was looming over the whole thing. *Was Terri really going to be ok?* I wasn't sure. *And if she wasn't ok, how in the world could her family go on without her?* I wasn't sure about that either. The kids seemed really shell shocked at Overland Park Regional. When I saw them in the waiting room, they were all sitting quietly in separate chairs apart from one another, as if each of them were in their own little glass boxes, dazed and silent. I was used to them climbing all over each other, close and jovial. Seeing them this way was such a far cry from their happy sibling reverie. It was disconcerting. I told them everything would be all right, but I couldn't imagine how they could possibly deal with the worst-case scenario. I prayed they wouldn't have to.

I woke disoriented to the phone ringing in the middle of the night. It was Mike. Terri's condition was continuing to worsen, and they were moving her to another hospital. He was following the ambulance.

Although he didn't say it, I *knew* he must've been overcome with fear. "Mike, let's just pray," was all I could think of to say. So we did. We prayed together and Mike asked me not to say anything to the kids in the morning. He wanted to be the one to relay the information to his children. Respectfully, I agreed, and somehow found a way to stall in the morning when the kids started asking questions until Mike could get there with some answers.

MIKE

Tests commenced right away once Terri arrived at the second hospital. CAT scans, CT scans, MRI's — all of them revealed worse results and more bad news than the one before. Terri had suffered six different strokes resulting in an undetermined amount of brain damage. She had a collapsed lung and untold internal injuries, but despite all that, she was fairly stable early Tuesday morning. Terri's sister, Tracy, was the first family member to arrive from out of town, and she tried to get a little food in Terri that morning. The nurses did some cognitive testing to determine the extent of brain function, and for a little while, we were optimistic.

My sister Margaret and my brother John and his wife, Lisa, flew in from Oregon. They swooped in and took charge of the household, directing things on the home front so that I could be at the hospital. They were joined by an army of friends who kept our family's routine running smoothly and as normal as possible for the kids. Meals started arriving hand over fist, and prayers were being offered non-stop. At one point, the entire Catholic grade school our younger children attended gathered together to pray the Rosary for Terri. The thought of hundreds of children and teachers uniting in prayer for our family and for Terri's recovery was truly awesome. God was pouring out His love in abundance, it was vastly evident everywhere I looked.

KAITLYN

My family is complicated, loud, and loving....an "in your face" kind of love that is full of emotion and dialogue. It's beautiful. And it's a little much sometimes for someone like me who's on the introverted side. I need to have my space and prefer to be left alone, so sometimes in this big, crazy, messy, wonderful family, I feel overwhelmed. But they're still *my* family. I mean, I would not trade them for the whole world. I loved growing up in this family. It was joyful and free – all my siblings played together, and we all got along. I was in charge, of course, but we had so much fun using our imaginations and just being together. I never dreamed that this happy ideal could be smashed to bits, but that's exactly what was happening. The tightly woven tapestry of our perfect little life was starting to unravel. My mom's accident was just the beginning.

Unbeknownst to anyone, I went by myself to visit my mom on Tuesday afternoon. I needed to see her, and I needed information. I had spoken with the doctors the night before, and it made me feel better, more at ease. I am a pragmatist – I need facts and information. That's what soothes me, so I ventured way out of my comfort zone, driving almost twenty miles from my neighborhood to the second hospital in two days to make sure for myself that my mom was really okay.

By the time I got there, she was not okay. I don't even remember anyone else being around. They probably were, but in my mind, it was just me and my mom, and she was freaking out. She kept saying she couldn't see anything and she was flailing and crying hysterically. I have never been so frightened in all my life, and the worst part was that there was absolutely nothing I could do.

MIKE

Throughout the day, we needed more and more of those prayers from our community as Terri's condition rapidly and mysteriously worsened.

She was in and out of consciousness and less and less responsive. A plethora of doctors visited her — teams of attending physicians with residents in tow, asking them for their insight and what they thought should be done. Despite all the attention, there was very little actually being done. It felt like Terri was just another case study — *Hey med students, take a look at this! This is what it looks like when someone is hit by a car, suffers multiple strokes, and starts to die from her injuries.* That is not the story I wanted to tell, but it was quickly becoming the narrative being written, and I was scared.

Terri had always been incredibly close with her sister, Tracy, and so it just followed that I was also close to her. I considered her *my* sister. When I had originally spoken to her the day before, I told her there was no need to come. She said she was coming anyway, and I was relieved she did. She resembles Terri in every aspect — the way she looks, the way she thinks, the way she speaks — there was something oddly comforting her being there because in a strange way, it felt like Terri was there helping me through this. Tracy and I took turns sitting by Terri's bedside. I did not want her to be alone even for a minute. We also took turns breaking down. I reassured her while she cried, and when I said, "God's gonna take her; He always takes the good ones, and I can't do this without her," she reassured me. She even made the difficult phone call to her parents to tell them they needed to come. Luckily, Terri's mom was already booked on a flight and scheduled to arrive later that day, but Tracy's call prompted Terri's dad and two brothers to make arrangements as soon as possible.

As the hours stretched on and into the next day, I grew more and more frustrated and finally angry. It had been two days at that point since the accident, but it felt like years. I had barely eaten or slept, and I had lost all track of time. It seemed as if we were starting to lose Terri, and no one was doing anything — I wanted answers and action, and I wanted it immediately.

LYNN

Utter chaos. COMPLETE and utter chaos — that's the best way I can describe the scene when I arrived to see Terri. There were plenty of doctors — too many doctors — but no one seemed to be in charge. There was no nucleus. Everyone was coming in and out, doing their own thing, but no one knew what anyone else was doing, and so ultimately, they ended up not doing anything to help Terri, who by that point, was declining fast. I was angry and frustrated. *Somebody do something!*

As the chaos raged on around us, Mike said, "Man, Lynn…God is really rockin' my boat right now."

"No!" I emphatically replied. "It's not God rocking your boat. It's Satan! Don't let him in. You have to be strong. You have to pray!"

In that instant, Mike turned and headed toward a cabinet on the other side of the room. He knelt down and literally almost put himself inside the cabinet. I'm not sure what he was doing, but I assume he was trying to physically protect himself from the barrage of darkness and doubt attacking him. He stayed that way for a while, deep in prayer. I don't know what happened in that cabinet, but when he emerged, he was completely calm and resolved that he would do whatever he needed to do to save Terri.

MIKE

Consulting by phone with Dr. Camarata, who was still in Chicago, Bob Thompson continued to offer advice and helped translate all the medical jargon into language that made sense. They both believed that the best course of action was to thin Terri's blood and increase her blood pressure, which would result in more blood flow to her brain. Bob was concerned that she was not getting enough, or possibly any, blood to her brain. The doctors assigned to Terri did not agree that that was the best course of action, so they were not willing to take the risk. It *was* risky, but at least it was action. They did not want to do *anything* until she stabilized, so that's what happened – absolutely nothing!

Bob gently nudged me along, reminding me about Dr. Camarata at St. Luke's. Certainly, he would be back soon. Bob had his number. *Should I call him?* That would mean another move. *Did that even make sense? Would Terri survive a move at this point?* All questions with no clear answers. The only thing I did feel certain about was that Bob was right. He said if we waited until Terri was stable, it would be too late. He did not consider the risk of moving her to be that great compared to the risk of leaving her where she was – he said she needed attention, and she needed it now!

"There is no way she will survive a move like that," her doctors were adamant on this point. If Terri stayed put, she might die. If Terri was moved, she might die. Terri dying was not an acceptable option, so I had to do something. Trusting Bob, I decided to call Dr. Camarata. Although I knew who Paul Camarata was because we attended the same church, I did not know him well. What I *did* know, however, was that he was a man of deep faith, precisely the kind of man I wanted and needed to try to save my wife.

He agreed to authorize Terri's transfer to St. Luke's and fly back to Kansas City immediately. He promised me that he would not only lead the team of doctors, but that he would be Terri's personal advocate, making every decision that needed to be made in her best interest. All I had to do was find a doctor who would talk to him on the phone to make the arrangements. As I wandered the halls searching for anyone who could help me, I grew more and more impatient. Every minute I spent trying to find someone was one more minute that Terri was slipping away.

KAY

When Mike first called on Monday right after Terri's accident, he said she was going to be fine and that she had not even broken any bones. Of course, Allan and I were worried, but so relieved to hear that she didn't sustain any significant injuries. Imagine our shock when Tracy called the following day and said, "It's serious. You and Dad need to come."

Now, my mother's intuition had already told me I needed to get there, so I booked a flight prior to Tracy's call, but there was something about hearing those words on the other end of the line. I can't describe the thoughts and emotions that go through a mother's mind and heart when she receives that kind of news. It doesn't matter how old your children are – they're *your* children, and the thought of losing them shatters you to the core. The hours between Tracy's call and my flight out of Utah were excruciating. To compound matters, my husband, Allan, was not able to fly out with me on Tuesday, and later was unable to get on any flights out. Just when he was about to give up hope of getting to Kansas City at all, his boss offered to fly him and our son David on his private plane free of charge. Repeatedly throughout this ordeal, we experienced God's loving care through the profound goodness of other people – this was just the beginning.

During my flight, I clutched religious medals that had belonged to Allan's mother, and I prayed. While I did not belong to any church or profess any formal religion, I *did* have a profound belief in the existence and goodness of God, and I *did* pray. Pinned in my seat for the two-and-a-half-hour flight, I prayed harder than I had probably ever prayed, pleading with God to let Terri be all right. I told Him we just can't lose her yet. My head was spinning, not knowing what was happening nor what to expect once I arrived, so I just kept praying.

When I got to the hospital and saw Terri, I was shocked. She didn't look like my Terri. She was so badly bruised and completely non-responsive. I didn't know what to think – I had never experienced anything quite like this before. As the day wore on and Terri's condition worsened, it became evident that we might lose her. I couldn't have that. Not my Terri. Not my beautiful, first-born baby. Terri had been such a good little girl, precocious, adorable, and a real sweetheart. When she was young, she loved taking care of her siblings, and as she grew up, she continued to be a "mother" in many ways even before giving birth to her own children. And what a truly excellent mother she was to my five fabulous grandchildren! She had a way of keeping everyone and everything organized and on track. There was no way they could lose her.

As Mike was busy trying to make decisions and track down doctors, I stood silently by Terri's bed, and in that moment, *I* made a decision. I knew that for fifteen long years, Terri had been praying persistently that I would become a Catholic. During my forty-six-year marriage to Allan, who was Catholic, we had never spoken much about me converting to Catholicism. He always told me it was up to me, and whatever I wanted to do was fine with him. We raised our children Catholic, but that was pretty much the extent of it for me. Standing there, holding Terri's hand and staring down at her broken body, I knew. I knew this was the right decision and this was the right time. I leaned in close and whispered in her ear, "Terri, I believe you can hear me. I want you to know that if you will be my sponsor and walk with me down the aisle to be baptized, I will become a Catholic." Now, I can't say that the heavens opened or the walls trembled, but what I can say, with all certainty, is that once I spoke those words, I felt my daughter squeeze my hand. I know she heard me, and I know that is one of the many reasons she fought so hard to come back to us.

MIKE

It had been a little more than forty-eight hours since I made the first phone call to Terri's parents, and by this point, her entire family had arrived. Her sister flew out immediately, followed shortly after by her mom. As it became clearer that Terri might not make it, her dad, Allan, and two brothers, David and Trip, joined them. Terri's dad later revealed that he was convinced he was flying to Kansas City to bury his beloved first-born daughter. When I asked him what he thought I should do in regard to moving Terri, he said, "She's your wife. It's your call."

I know how difficult that was for him. As a father, I also know all too well how hard it was for him to surrender his protective, fatherly nature and trust me completely with the decision-making. She was still his little girl, and he was crushed at the thought of losing her. "This isn't how it's supposed to be," he said. "I'm supposed to go first."

Strangely, I felt a great sense of peace about my decision to move Terri. God is good and gave me such a strong resolve at that moment. I knew that I had to do anything and everything I possibly could to save her. Once I finally found a doctor willing to speak with Paul Camarata, the transfer happened at lightning speed. Within the hour, I was riding with Terri in an ambulance to the third hospital in three days, praying non-stop for a miracle.

Chapter 3

THY WILL BE DONE

"We have this confidence in Him, that if we ask anything according to His will, He hears us."

1 JOHN 5:14

DR. BOB THOMPSON

When I arrived at the first hospital on Monday, Terri's condition was quickly disintegrating from bad to worse. When she was moved to St. Luke's in the wee hours of the morning on Thursday, I honestly thought we were losing her. What was incredibly scary to see was the way she was posturing. Her arms were bent in toward her body, with her wrists and fingers stiff and held to her chest. This was indicative of the fact that her cerebral cortex was no longer functioning, meaning the brain stem had taken over. This kind of cerebral dysfunction is not compatible with living long. I was worried she was not going to make it. I told Mike it didn't look good and that he should go ahead and call the kids — they needed to be there in case it was time to say good-bye.

MIKE

Devastation. That's what I felt when Bob told me I should send for the kids. Utter devastation and a complete loss of any strand of hope to which I had been clinging. *This is it. This is it. This is how it's going to end, right here tonight, right now. I made the decision to move her and that is precisely what is going to kill her.* I fell apart. Literally. Fell to my knees and then to the floor, curled up like a baby in my brother John's arms, and cried my eyes out. This was pain and fear like I had never known. It came from a deep, guttural place where I felt like my soul was being ripped from my body. I cried so hard and so long that there were no more tears left — just a silent heaving that racked every single bone in my body. Terri was a part of me. *How could I lose her? How could I live without her?* I couldn't.

John just held me and let me lose it. Terri's brother, David, looked on with concern. He had never seen me like this, and he was afraid the kids were going to walk in any minute and see me in this shattered state. I knew I needed to get it together, but in that moment, I felt like I was drowning and had absolutely no strength left to pull myself to the surface.

COURTNEY

Auntie Lisa was at our house, and Kaitlyn and I had stayed up late talking with her in the kitchen. She was so much fun, and I loved hanging out with her. I don't know what time we finally went to bed, but it couldn't have been very long before I heard the phone ring. Immediately after that, Auntie Lisa was waking us up and telling us to get John Milton, Halley, and Abby up and dressed. She told us our mom's condition had worsened and that we needed to go to the hospital to tell her good-bye. I'd like to say that at that moment I stepped up and took care of my siblings, but I didn't. Kaitlyn did, but I completely broke down. I lost it and could not get it back together. This was so big, so scary, so overwhelming. All I could do was cry.

We rushed to the car. Kaitlyn held and soothed Halley, who was barely awake, and I cried quietly next to John Milton and frantically flipped through my Bible. Everyone else was silent.

MIKE

As I was breaking down, our five beautiful children rounded the corner, and I knew that I had no choice — I had to be strong for them. I cannot explain how I instantaneously picked myself up except to say that it had to have been the work of the Holy Spirit. I went from a heap on the floor to the calm, cool, and collected head of my family in the blink of an eye. If there was ever a time in my life when I was thankful for the Holy Spirit showing up, this was it!

I explained to the kids what was happening and that it was very possible that their mother might not pull through this. These are words you never imagine yourself saying to your young children. I had had difficult conversations with them before, but there had never been a more formidable discussion than this. I remained strong and emphasized the importance of faith and the power of prayer. At least, that's what I tried to do. Truth be told, Terri was the positive one in our relationship and certainly had far more faith than I did. She would have done a stellar job delivering this news to our family. She would have been the rock they had all come to depend on for spiritual and emotional strength. She would have handled all of this so much better than I did. Half of me was trying to remain calm and help the kids digest it all, and the other half of me couldn't stop thinking, *How the hell can I do this alone?*

ABBY

When my aunt woke me up, I was so disoriented. I didn't know what time it was or what was happening. She told me to get dressed, and in my confusion, I put on my soccer uniform. I remember standing on the stairs and hearing Courtney say, "Mom might die tonight." *WHAT!* It felt like a slap in the face. As we drove through the darkness, my brain understood why we were heading to the hospital in the middle of the night, but my heart was too broken to take in this new reality.

When we arrived, the sheer number of family members there was not only overwhelming, but a tell-tale sign of the fact that this was as bad as I had feared. It was not a nightmare; it was real, and I knew that the ending was not going to be good. I was not going to be surprised this time though because tonight, I knew in my gut, that the worst-case scenario *was* going to happen. Even if it didn't happen tonight, I felt sure that my mom was going to die. I did not want to talk to anyone, and I certainly did not want to pray about it. I wasn't ready, and I felt so hopeless and helpless that I didn't think it mattered anyway.

MIKE

While Terri's life hung in the balance, Dr. Camarata and his team were preparing to perform a diagnostic procedure to assess whether there was any blood flow to Terri's brain. The procedure itself was incredibly risky, but without it, there was no way for the doctors to accurately determine the scope of the damage. There was already a sizable chance that Terri wouldn't make it, but the risks associated with *any* procedures tipped the scales even further in that direction. At least we were all together. If something happened, we were all there. Everyone was in the loop as far as what was going on, and we could support one another. While we waited, the kids and I and all our family and friends who were gathered joined in a circle and prayed the Rosary. We prayed for healing for Terri, for the doctors who were treating her, and ultimately for God's will to be done. That's not an easy prayer to say when you're not sure that His will is going to parallel your will. It was a powerful prayer experience and a moment of real surrender for me. Terri was in God's hands, and I could trust that His will was far more perfect than my own.

DR. PAUL CAMARATA

I was shocked at the shape Terri was in when she arrived at St. Luke's. She was only minimally responsive to painful stimulus and posturing with her extremities, which indicated to me that her brainstem was not receiving enough blood. Her scans showed multiple strokes on both sides of her brain, some of them quite large. It looked as though it would be impossible for her to survive without significant impairments to her sight and movement. That is, if she were to survive at all! Her blood pressure was low; she had no invasive blood pressure monitoring and was on no medication to increase her blood pressure or thin her blood. She had been in the hospital for several days with bilateral dissections of her carotid arteries, but had not yet had a cerebral arteriogram, an invasive test where contrast dye is injected directly into the arteries to the brain to see which vessels are narrowed or blocked and which might need to be opened with a stent.

Seeing her terrible neurologic condition, I knew we had to act fast. Although it was almost midnight, we mobilized our team quickly. The first step was to place an arterial catheter to continuously monitor her blood pressure. We then started Terri on medicine to artificially raise her blood pressure to perfuse the brain better and then immediately took her for a cerebral arteriogram. This was a risky procedure, but necessary. I knew that Terri might not survive it, but I also knew it was our best shot at determining the best course of action. I wanted to do everything in my power to figure out what was happening so that we could try to save Terri's life. That being said, I understood that as a doctor, my powers only extended so far. At some point, I had to put it in God's hands, so as we began the arteriogram, that is precisely what I did. I prayed.

JOHN MILTON

On Monday afternoon, when we had pulled into the driveway after school and seen my dad, I thought he had come home early to surprise us with a trip or something really cool, but at St. Luke's, I understood that my mom might die. *How can your entire life change so quickly?* I thought we were going to Disney World just a couple days ago, and now here we were in a hospital in the middle of the night to tell our mom good-bye. Seeing my "BopBop" (my mom's dad) and all my mom's family there made it sink in. I knew if they had all flown in, it must be pretty bad.

I am a realist. I was a realist even then at the age of eleven. I didn't like to sugar coat things and I didn't like it when others did either. Things are the way they are. Better to deal with it head on. Nothing we did or didn't do was going to change the outcome for my mom, so all the praying really didn't matter.

MIKE

After what felt like an eternity, Dr. Camarata emerged with an update. The arteriogram revealed good news and bad news. The bad news was that both of Terri's carotid arteries had been dissected. These are the two major arteries responsible for supplying oxygenated blood to the brain. The good news was that a smaller artery in the back of her head – the vertebral artery – kicked into overdrive and was supplying larger than normal amounts of blood to her brain. Dr. Camarata called it a miracle and believed that Terri might just have a chance. *Oh God, if this is your will...thank you!*

HALLEY

When you're the youngest, everyone treats you differently. I was only six when my mom had her accident, so everyone was trying to protect me, but I understood what was happening, and I remember much of it. That night at St. Luke's, I just wanted to break free and run away. This was what I had feared from the moment I first saw my mom after the accident. I hadn't even recognized her and had burst into tears immediately, thinking to myself, *I won't have a mom anymore!* Everyone had tried to console me by telling me she would be all right. Now, my worst fears were coming true – everyone was saying she was going to die. I didn't want to say good-bye to my mom!

While everyone was saying the Rosary, I said a little prayer to God all by myself in the silence of my heart, and when Dr. Camarata came out to talk to us, I knew my prayer had been answered. I don't even think it *was* Dr. Camarata who came out to tell us my mom was going to be okay. I think it was truly God, and I think He was giving my mom another chance because there was more He wanted her to do. He knew we needed her, and He needed her to be our mom at least a little while longer.

COURTNEY

Finally, after an excruciating wait, my dad came in with Dr. Camarata. I listened as he said my mom would make it through the night, and I remember hearing the word "stabilized." At that, I ran toward Dr. Camarata and hugged him! Everyone was hugging each other and laughing with relief, but honestly, although I did feel some degree of consolation, I still harbored a little skepticism. How could Dr. Camarata know with absolute certainty that my mom would make it to the morning? I desperately wanted to see my mom, but they wouldn't allow it. They said she needed complete rest and quiet. I felt angry that I was not able to see her at that point because in my mind, I couldn't trust that things would not take a turn for the worse again throughout the night. I didn't want to leave without seeing her, but that's how it had to be.

ABBY

I was certain that when I saw the doctor, the look on his face would tell me everything I needed to know, but I was not prepared for what I saw on Dr. Camarata's face. He seemed almost confused, like even *he* couldn't believe what he was telling us. Obviously, he didn't expect the good news either.

The worst part of that night was having to leave without seeing my mom. We went, expecting to tell her good-bye, so it was weirdly anti-climactic to not even get to see her at all, even though we were relieved at the new outlook we had been given.

The best part of that night was camping out in the living room with my siblings and my aunt, watching the musical *Hairspray* and singing all the songs. Aunt Lisa was amazing! She knew just what to do to take our minds off what was happening. There was tremendous comfort in being with my siblings. *That* was normal. *That* was how things should be. Everyone played their respective roles, and *that* is something I could count on. In the midst of all this craziness, it felt good to laugh and to know I wasn't alone.

MIKE

Dr. Camarata felt hopeful that Terri had a chance, but he was very clear about the fact that there was no way to know what the quality of her life would be from this point forward. There had been brain damage for sure, the extent of which was still unknown. He also emphasized the fact that the brain is a funny thing – unpredictable. People heal differently. Terri's injuries could have killed her. The fact that she was still holding on to life was nothing short of miraculous, but that did not necessarily mean she would experience a full recovery. It did not mean she would experience *any* substantial recovery. There was no way to know. He said I should prepare myself for the chance that she could be in a vegetative state for a very long time, maybe forever. He said we could potentially be looking at a permanent nursing home situation if she did not regain significant cognitive and physical function.

I didn't know how to feel. Obviously, I felt relief at the doctor's words that Terri had a chance at survival, but my heart sank when he said he did not know what her quality of life would be like. His words, "permanent nursing home" sounded almost as bad as a death sentence. *Was this the miracle I had prayed for? Was this God's will? Why wouldn't He have just taken her when we thought we were losing her anyway?* I walked a fine line with God between gratitude and bitterness, hope and disbelief. Through it all, the words that Jesus Himself gave us kept echoing in my heart, "*Thy will be done.*" I just kept praying that His will was an even bigger miracle than we had already witnessed, but I would have to be patient. The doctors said Terri could be in the ICU for months.

Chapter 4

TRYING TO PICK UP THE PIECES

"I can do all things through Christ who gives me strength."

PHILIPPIANS 4:13

MIKE

We weren't out of the woods yet. Terri made it through that night, but there were still issues. Because she was an avid runner, she had very low blood pressure. While that is not unusual for a runner, in this case, it meant that not as much blood was getting to Terri's brain and not as quickly as they would like it to. Just as Bob had suggested, Dr. Camarata wanted to thin her blood and increase her blood pressure, allowing as much blood to be pumped to her brain as quickly as possible. While this sounded like a reasonable approach, it came with great risks. Increasing Terri's blood pressure would increase the internal bleeding from her other injuries and she could bleed out.

There I was with yet another decision. This could save her, or it could kill her. I asked Dr. Camarata for his advice, and he said with certainty, "If it were my wife, I would try to save her brain."

That was all I needed to hear. I gave the go ahead, and they gave Terri Coumadin and Heparin to thin her blood. As anticipated, this triggered a series of other issues. The internal bleeding became a problem because now that her blood was thinner, it was like she had a garden hose full of holes inside her. She was bleeding from multiple areas and needed numerous transfusions. She had a severe allergic reaction to the Heparin, needed a surgical procedure to stop the enormous hematoma growing in her abdomen, had to have a tracheotomy tube inserted, and was put on a ventilator.

As it continued to unfold, all we could do was pray, and wait... wait, and pray...and try, somehow, to pick up where we had left off several days before. Our normal lives and routines had been shattered to pieces and replaced with something so strange, surreal, and unrecognizable. Picking those pieces up and trying to put it all back together wasn't easy. The words of my mom's favorite Bible verse, "I can do all things through Christ who gives me strength," have never rung more true in my heart than during this crisis. There is absolutely no way I could have even remained on my feet from moment to moment without the sheer grace of God bracing me up and the tremendous outpouring of support and help from our family, neighbors, friends, and fellow Church of the Nativity parishioners. God is so good, and when I most needed to see Him and feel His presence, He manifested Himself in an army of loving caretakers – some of them I didn't even know! They rallied around our family, buoyed us up, and literally carried us through the darkest hours when we were not sure if Terri would survive. Three of Terri's friends, Lynn, Elizabeth, and Coleen, stepped in and began handling things I didn't even know needed to be handled. They came to be known affectionately by our family as the "three amigos," but it probably would've been more apropos to call them the "three angels." Even after we knew that Terri was going to make it, they continued to lavish us with love and support beyond measure.

LYNN

Terri is ridiculously organized. She had running a household with five children down to a science. It was a well-oiled machine. Stepping in and trying to fill her shoes was a formidable challenge, a downright almost impossible one, because it took us a while to decipher her very complex calendar. Five kids, five different schedules, various colors, numerous abbreviations…it was truly an elaborate code to be broken, but once we figured it out, we were in business. While Mike's brother and his wife kept the inner workings of the house and family running smoothly, Coleen Weller, Elizabeth Crawford, and I divvied up the additional responsibilities making sure that meals were provided and that everyone got where they needed to be at the right time on the right day.

There was comfort in control. I could control a meal schedule and a carpool schedule, but I could not control what was happening to Terri, and in those first few days, it was touch and go. The first time I saw her at St. Luke's in the ICU, I could not believe that was really her. She was hooked up to more machines than I could count with all sorts of tubes and wires attached. *This can't be. This may not end well.* I continued to have that uneasy feeling I had the very first night following the accident. The giant question mark was still shrouding everything in doubt – would Terri be okay? Friends and neighbors called me to ask if they should go see her – if they *needed* to go see her because she wasn't going to make it. As much as I wanted to believe that she was going to be fine, I had a difficult time answering them because doubt kept creeping in around the edges of my heart. So I just kept praying.

COLEEN

I knew Elizabeth, but not well, and I had never even met Lynn, but there the three of us were, riffling through Terri's kitchen drawers and cabinets. We were trying desperately to find any information that might clue us in to Terri's elaborate organizational system and the kids' busy schedules. I was uncomfortable invading someone else's privacy that way, but we were driven by a panicked urgency – we *had* to figure things out to keep the family running. Our sole focus was maintaining as much normalcy for the kids as we possibly could, and we were bound and determined to make that happen, even if it meant snooping in files, drawers, cabinets, and computer documents.

While the three of us managed carpools and meal deliveries, we also became increasingly intentional about protecting the kids, and later, Terri's parents, Kay and Allan, too. People are well meaning, but sometimes, in their good intentions, they say things they shouldn't, they cross boundaries, and sometimes, it's just too much. When you're going through a crisis, there are times you need a little space. Lynn, Elizabeth, and I saw this, and we tried very hard to act as a buffer for the family. We fielded questions as best we could and relayed information when there was news, but mainly we wanted to create a safe space for the family, an oasis of peace amid the utter chaos that raged around them.

MIKE

In those first few days, my brother John and his wife, Lisa, moved into the house to care for the kids so that I could stay at the hospital 24/7. John tackled the mounting stack of mail and unpaid bills. Terri was in charge of running the household and there was so much that only she knew. Figuring it all out was like finding pieces of a puzzle and trying to fit them together. In retrospect, there were some funny moments, like when John said, "You only have eight in the checking account."

"Eight hundred?" I asked.

"No, eight dollars!"

"Are you kidding me?"

Interjecting concern, Terri's dad asked if we needed money. I reassured him we had put money aside for a rainy day, to which he replied, "Rainy day? This is a damn deluge!"

As it turned out, Terri had written a rather large check to the IRS the morning of the accident and had planned to transfer money from our savings account to cover it, but she never got the chance. Things like that kept coming up, things that Terri handled, but now, in her absence, I had to figure out. It was a constant reminder of how quickly life can change. You go out for a run one morning and you end up in the hospital unable to pick up where you left off.

Lisa did a great job keeping the kids' spirits up and things functioning as close to normal as possible. My sister Margaret was my rock, staying with me at a hotel near the hospital and making sure I was taking care of myself. She started a journal to keep track of Terri's progress. She titled it, "Road to Recovery." Apparently, she never had any doubt that Terri was going to make it. Her optimism, along with everyone else's, was a blessing.

If there was one person I know I couldn't have survived without, it would be Terri's sister, Tracy. A professional event planner, she is never afraid to take her gloves off and dig in no matter the situation. This was no exception. She got busy right away, wrapping towels and placing them under Terri's head and massaging her atrophied right hand. Tracy was the vital link between me and what was going on at home. She communicated with Lisa and then passed on whatever I needed to know. I'm sure she probably filtered some things that she thought perhaps I didn't need to (or couldn't) deal with at the time. A strong woman both physically and emotionally, she quickly became my confidant in those early days.

JOHN MILTON

We got talked TO a lot in the days immediately following my mom's accident. I know that I didn't process most of it – I didn't want to. It was all too hard, too sad, and too scary. People kept saying things like, "Keep praying, she'll pull through." That was nice, but it didn't provide me with *any* solace because I knew we had no control over what would or would not happen.

I just wanted everything to go back to "normal," and really, that hope of normalcy was the only thing that gave me any comfort. Talking with my sisters and hanging out with my friends made me feel like all was right with the world. Being the only boy with four sisters wasn't always easy, but I would not trade it. Of course, I always wished I had a "bro," but as children, Abby and I were playmates – she did boy stuff with me, and I did girl stuff with her, so it all worked out. Although I was closest to Abby as kids, I am far more similar to Kaitlyn, and as this situation unfolded, she and I had many conversations that revealed just how much on the same page we really were. Through everything, we all grew closer and pulled together, but sometimes we pushed each other away too as we were all dealing with this in our own separate and unique ways.

HALLEY

I had nightmares about my mom every single night. I remembered her long hair, how I would run with her, and her beautiful voice as she sang to me at bedtime. I missed her and wanted her back! There was a picture of her on the wall in my room, and I would sing to it and pray every day, but the nightmares still came.

ABBY

The weirdest thing in the day or two following our nighttime trek to St. Luke's was that everyone thought my mom had died.

Apparently, word had spread that she was fading fast, so people just assumed we had lost her. Friends kept calling to say they were sorry. I guess I should have felt this profound relief in being able to say she was alive, but I felt too overcome with fear and doubt. We went to the hotel where my dad was staying to swim and spend some time with him.

"We're not out of the woods yet" was what he told us. *What does that mean?* I felt angsty, like we were all just waiting for the other shoe to drop. Our emotions were raw, so raw that I found it difficult to express what was going on in my mind and heart.

COURTNEY

We had always looked to Kaitlyn as our fearless leader, and true to form, she took care of us and worked extremely hard to maintain peace in the household. She would help me with anything I asked and packed all our lunches. She so fluidly stepped into the maternal role I hardly noticed how much she was doing. I was not nearly as much help to my family as she was.

I had a great deal of pent up anger. I just wanted things to get back to "normal," and the more I realized there was no such thing as "normal" anymore, the more frustrated and disappointed I became. I was so sad that my mom missed my production of *Godspell* – it was my first musical. After every performance, I would tell myself that my mom was going to wake up in time to see it, but that time didn't come.

Going back to school was strange. *How did so many people know what had happened?* As an awkward high schooler, I didn't want all this attention directed at me. People were nice, but I just wanted to go to school to escape from my reality for a while. I had tunnel vision – I wanted to plow ahead and not deal with everything going on around me.

KAITLYN

I had always been the "mom" when we played house, and I often played that role in real life with my siblings as well, so it was just natural for me to step up and into my mother's shoes. *Who else was going to do it?* I was the oldest. I was the only one who could drive. No one else understood the inner workings of our household and family better than I did, so it just made sense. No one asked this of me, but I *wanted* to do it. I wanted to keep things running and hold it all together, just like my mom did every single day. So that's what I did. I grew up fast, took charge, and accepted responsibility. In retrospect, it took a toll on me for sure, but would I change it? Not in a million years. Chauffeuring my siblings around, making lunches, running errands…it all helped me to feel in control of a situation over which I had absolutely zero.

The worst part was going back to school. Everyone, of course, asked about my mom and wanted to know what was going on. I, of course, did not want to talk about it and just tried to lay low. One day, my guidance counselor called me out of class, and my mind immediately raced to the worst possible scenario. On the agonizing walk down the hall to his office, I was sure my mom had died and he was calling me down to the office to break the horrible news. Needless to say, I was a mess. When I got there, it turned out he was just checking on me and only wanted to chat. *Are you kidding me?* I mean, that was very thoughtful, but at the same time, considerably thought-less. In truly genuine attempts to help, people often made things so much worse.

On another day, a substitute teacher had us watch a video about a kid getting hit by a car. I lost it! I just got up, walked out of the building, and sat in my car and cried. No one understood how fragile we were, how expectantly we were all waiting for the bottom to drop out, how very close we all were at different times to completely falling apart.

Chapter 5

A WEEK OF SMALL BUT MIGHTY MIRACLES

"With God, all things are possible."

MARK 10:27

MIKE

As one day bled into the next, I felt like our prayers were slowly being answered. Every tick of the clock was another step toward more certainty of survival. When you're not sure if the woman you love is going to live another day, you look for and cling to any little sign of hope. Another MRI showed no further strokes, which meant Terri was stabilizing. The doctors began very gradually to decrease the dosage of sedatives they were administering to keep her calm and help her heal. On Saturday, May 3, just five days after the accident, I got the sign I needed. I recorded it in the journal Margaret started:

Terri, I prayed to the Father for one little sign that you are fighting to get well. It has been five days since I saw your beautiful eyes. My prayers were answered today when I walked into the room and you had your eyes wide open. As I began to talk to you, you turned your head toward me and smiled. It was just like I was looking at Jesus — the joy I felt could have only come from heaven.

The next day, Sunday, May 4, Terri's nurses washed and French braided her hair, put make-up on her, propped her up, and covered up all the tubes with blankets for the kids' first visit. I thought Terri looked absolutely beautiful! After their visit, she opened her eyes again, and the nurses confirmed that they saw a smile. How simple is a smile, and yet how much do we take a smile from our loved ones for granted? A tragedy like this certainly helps you put things in perspective. All the things you thought mattered don't anymore, and all the things you took for granted suddenly become immensely significant.

JOHN MILTON

I wanted to see my mom, but I hated seeing my mom when she was unconscious. I didn't understand why we visited her when she didn't even know what was happening. The number of machines was frightening, and she didn't even look like my mom — her hair was different and they put too much make-up on her. It seemed cruel to see her when she was so not herself.

COURTNEY

I was told that the nurses were trying to make my mom look "normal" to help Halley feel more comfortable, but I remember thinking that this was pointless. *She's already in a hospital with a ton of tubes and machines, and she will not wake up if we talk to her. Who are we trying to fool?* Halley was very young at the time though, so it was a kind gesture, but for me, it was just another reminder that I was quickly losing my mother. It wasn't her in the bed, no matter how much it looked like her. This was some mannequin that had taken her place, and my real mother was gone.

MIKE

The roller coaster of emotions we were all riding was dizzying. Just days before, I was sure I was going to lose Terri, and now, I felt certain she was going to make it. The scary part was not knowing exactly what that was going to look like. I was fairly certain that we would be in for a new "normal," but I kept praying that God's will would be for a full and total recovery. The doctors told me that I could gauge the progress of Terri's condition by the number of machines and tubes she was connected to. They said that a sure sign of improvement was when a machine or tube was disconnected, so that became my barometer — how many machines there were from one day to the next. And there *was* progress, slow and steady, but progress just the same.

In the days that followed, Terri continued to open her eyes, track movement, and blink in answer to direct questions. An angiogram revealed good blood flow to the brain and improved blood flow in the damaged blood vessels. She was removed from the ventilator, and her feeding tube was moved to her abdomen which made it easier to get nutrition to her.

Terri's sister, Tracy, sat by her bedside for hours and read scripture to her, which seemed to soothe Terri. She couldn't speak because of the tracheotomy, and her hands and legs didn't work, but she could stick out her tongue and blink. Tracy would say, "Stick out your tongue if you want me to read more," and Terri would stick out her tongue. The problem was that Terri would stick out her tongue even when she hadn't been asked a question — it made for some comical moments, which were good for all of us.

By the end of that week, Terri was sitting in a chair for up to six hours and trying very hard to interact, although still unable to speak. Her exceptional nurses continued to go above and beyond, one even coming in on her day off to visit and check on her. They went all out to get Terri bathed, fixed up, and sitting up for a special visit from the kids that Thursday. Terri's face lit up immediately when they walked into the room, and to everyone's surprise and delight, she mouthed the name of our youngest, Halley. The joy and relief I felt at this tiny action was overwhelming. One of my biggest fears was that Terri might not remember the kids. This moment was huge! I knew that Terri —*my* Terri — was in there somewhere, and I felt more hopeful than ever that the full recovery I had prayed for was truly possible.

HALLEY

As much as I wanted my mom, I was scared to visit her in the hospital. I didn't like all the machines, and I didn't like that my mom didn't look like my mom. Before we went in that Thursday, they told us that they weren't sure if she would recognize us – that made me even more scared to go in, but all my fears were relieved when I saw my mom mouth my name. MY name! She knew me! She knew ME! I was so happy that God was answering our prayers. I think He knew that my dad needed my mom, that we ALL needed her.

ABBY

I *wanted* to see my mom, but it was difficult to see my mom. I was sad not seeing her, but I was sad when I *did* see her. It was a difficult balance. When we got the word that she was starting to "wake up," I didn't even think about the fact that she might not remember us, so when they stopped us at her door to warn us, I was completely taken aback. *Not remember us? Seriously? Why did the worst-case scenario possibilities keep surprising me?* The thought of her being awake but not recognizing us terrified me. I didn't think I could deal with that. I didn't want to go in. I would rather not see her and not know versus see her and find out that our faces ignited no spark of recognition. *Oh God, why would you let her live this way? If this is the way it's gonna be, why didn't you just take her?* I knew I had to go in, and in a split second, my worst fears were dispelled as I saw the glimmer of recognition in my mom's eyes. That would have been enough, but to see her actually mouth Halley's name – that was remarkable.

MIKE

It's funny how life goes on. It hadn't even been two weeks since Terri's accident – *my* life felt like it was at a standstill – but everyone else's around me seemed to be moving forward. I guess that's as it should be. My brother and his wife had to get back home for the grandchild they were expecting any day. Terri's sister had to get home after leaving her husband to man the ship for the last eleven days. As family slowly started returning to their own lives, I quickly realized how much help I was going to need. Although Terri was making beautiful progress, the doctors were still saying she could be in the ICU for a while and on a stroke floor after that for months. The next step would be an in-patient rehabilitation hospital for up to another six months and probably a day treatment program after that. We had a long road ahead of us, and I knew I couldn't be there for Terri the way she needed *and* be there for the kids the way they needed. After weighing several options, I asked Terri's parents if they would be willing to move in for the duration of Terri's recovery. Of course, they graciously agreed and went back to Utah for a few days to make arrangements and collect their necessities.

In yet another miraculous display of community, our dearest friends took great pains to make a welcoming space for my in-laws in our home. We didn't have a guest room or any extra furniture, and Kay and Allan didn't feel right about staying in our room. Family friends, Coleen and Rick Weller, donated a full bedroom set of furniture while others moved our piano room into the dining room and converted that space into a second master for Terri's parents. Lynn and Coleen even cut out little brown cardboard squares and taped them to each of the French door windowpanes so that Allan and Kay could have some privacy. I was blown away – every single time there was a need of any sort, people swooped in and took care of it. It was humbling and overwhelming, and a true testament to what Terri meant to the people in our neighborhood and in our church community.

LYNN

Making preparations for the "in-law suite" with Coleen was therapeutic. We were alone in the house and had the chance to talk about what had happened and how we were each processing it. I was beginning to feel a slight shift. The doubt that had pervaded my heart and mind at the beginning was slowly giving way to small slivers of hope. It was still hard for me to visit Terri in the ICU. Seeing her just lying there made me sad. That's not the Terri I knew, the strong, athletic woman who was always in control. I wanted so badly to be able to talk with her and to laugh the way we always did, to tell her how much I loved her. I sat by her bedside and continued to pray for her recovery.

I felt a great sense of peace about her being at St. Luke's. Mike was much calmer, and it was apparent that Dr. Camarata was in charge and that he and the nurses were taking excellent care of Terri. One night, I was in the waiting room with all of Mike and Terri's family, and like siblings do, they were teasing each other and giving each other a hard time. I heard a sound at that point that I had not heard much in the last week or so – laughter. They were laughing! That was the moment

I realized that there was some levity in this situation. That was the moment I realized that everything *was* really going to be okay.

KAY

Agreeing to move into Mike and Terri's home for the duration of Terri's recovery was a no-brainer for me. Mike said he *could* have the kids stay at various friends' houses, but his real desire was to keep them all together and to maintain as much normalcy as possible. He needed to be completely available to Terri, so of course we didn't even hesitate for one second when he asked if we would consider moving in. I can't imagine being home in Utah during Terri's recovery – I wanted to help, but also, selfishly, *I* wanted to be there. *I* needed to see Terri and to know exactly how she was doing from day to day.

I also knew that *she* needed me. When Terri's little sister, Tracy, was three years old, she was diagnosed with a frightening disease. Her body thought her very own blood was a virus, so it did what our bodies do, her immune system started attacking her blood cells. It was an extremely rare, extremely dangerous condition, and at one point, the doctors told us she was not going to survive it. In the throes of that crisis, *my* mother moved in with us to help with the other kids, and she often reminded me how important it was for me not to ignore my other children. I realize this was not exactly an identical situation, but I knew that Terri would want me there to make sure that *her* children got all the love and attention that she was unable to shower upon them at that time. And seeing Tracy there, sitting beside Terri's bed some thirty years later, was a glaringly beautiful reminder that doctors are often wrong.

MIKE

That Saturday, May 10, the kids had a special early Mother's Day gift for Terri. Lynn had taken them to Build-a-Bear the day before, and they selected the perfect bear, dressed him in an assortment of clothing and accessories that reflected each of their interests and personalities, and then recorded messages to place in his paws so that Terri could hear their voices anytime she wanted. It still holds a cherished spot in our home to this day.

The next day was Mother's Day, and after attending Mass, we all visited Terri. Her parents had arrived back in KC from Utah, and we gathered around her to read the Gospel for the day. Afterward, I gave her communion. Although she couldn't really eat it, I touched a tiny morsel to her lips. It was a very good day as Terri seemed happy to see us and genuinely attempted to communicate with us. It was hard to know what she was trying to say, but at least she was trying. As each small miracle unfolded that week, I was more and more grateful and more and more hopeful for the days and weeks to come.

Chapter 6

REMEMBERING

"Consider it all joy, my brothers, when you encounter various trials, for you know that the testing of your faith produces perseverance."

JAMES 1:2-3

TERRI

There was not one clear, defining moment when I "woke up." It happened gradually and the memories are fuzzy at best. I'm probably a little too quick to say I don't remember any of it, but when I carefully think about it, there are bits and pieces – glimpses – all the way back to the beginning. I don't remember seeing the kids at the first hospital, Overland Park Regional, but I do remember feeling scared there when I couldn't see or feel anything. I'm sure I was terrified, but what I remember more vividly than fear is how quickly it faded and was replaced with an overwhelming sense of peace. I can't explain why, I just remember I was ready to let go, and it wasn't frightening or panic-ridden. I wasn't worried. Just peace. I was thinking that if I could just go be with Jesus, then that would be fine with me. I feel badly admitting that now in a way because I don't want my family to think that I wasn't concerned about *them*, but in that moment, I was honestly ready to let it all go.

Once I realized – or God decided – that it was not my time, that's when I started fighting, and that's when I remember the panic kicking in. I was in pain, flailing, and I wanted more morphine. I remember my sister sitting by my bedside and her soothing voice reading scripture. I have glimpses of my best friend Lynn being there, and I remember my mom telling me she would be baptized a Catholic if I pulled through. I can't recall actual images of Mike, but I have a very definite sense that he was always there beside me.

There are memories of voices too. The most striking is Dr. Camarata's. When Mike asked him what he would do, I clearly heard him say, "If it were my wife, I would try to save her brain." That is my final memory before I started to come out of it several days later.

It's hard to say at that point what was real and what was not. Much of it felt like a dream, or a sort of semi-consciousness where what is actually happening is mingled with dreams to create a mish-mash of reality. Of course, I was disoriented, and I kept thinking to myself, "Was I really in the hospital the whole time?" For some reason, I had weird, cloudy memories of being in something like a mobile home or some sort of machine. I remember hearing a constant, mechanical tic-tic-tic, and it felt like I was being moved around a lot. *Where am I?* To compound this, St. Luke's was under construction at the time, so the view from my window was all machinery – cranes and bulldozers and construction material. There were even some paranoid moments when I thought, "Where does Mike have me? Am I really in the hospital?"

My earliest memory after "waking up" is a visit from the kids. On that day, the nurses hoisted me up to a sitting position using a harness because I couldn't hold my own body weight or even my head up by myself. It was incredibly humiliating as I realized I couldn't do *anything* by myself, and I was thinking, "*THIS* is pathetic. I'll just tell them to stop. I'll just tell them no," but I couldn't speak. I was thinking it, but because of the trach tube, I couldn't get any words to come out. I didn't understand they were getting me ready to see the kids, so I couldn't comprehend why in the world they were making me go through this rigmarole. I just wanted it to stop.

I can't say I remember the kids' visit that day all too clearly, but I do remember seeing them and mouthing Halley's name. My thoughts were crystal clear, and it was unbelievably frustrating not to be able to communicate in that moment with my children. I kept thinking, "They don't know.... they don't know how much I want to hug them.... they don't know how much I want to tell them I love them.... they don't know how much I want to say I'm sorry." I wanted desperately to apologize for putting them through this whole ordeal. I know the accident wasn't my fault, but I felt so badly that they were going through this because I knew it must've been wrenching for them. I'm the one who's supposed to make everything better for *them* when they're hurting. I'm the one who's supposed to worry about *them*. They're not supposed to have to worry about *me*. I'm not the one who's supposed to be lying here, helpless. My heart was heavy with sorrow and grief over the fear and anguish my condition had caused them. Everything was turned upside down, and I was convinced I could make it right if I could only talk.

There are glimpses of other visits from the kids. I remember the build-a-bear named "Faith" they gave me. I remember Mike's brother John and his wife Lisa's voice, but have no memory of actually seeing them, though I am certain they were there. I don't remember seeing my parents at this point either, but I know they were there too.

Mike brought me Jesus in the Eucharist almost every single day. He would place a tiny piece on my tongue and it would dissolve while he prayed the "Our Father" aloud. I wanted so badly to pray it with him, but I couldn't even find the words in my head. I had been praying this prayer for over forty years, and now I had forgotten it. That frightened me because I knew I *should* know it. Mike was my strength, and in prayer, he had now become my words. It gave a whole new meaning to "The two shall become one flesh." What a blessing that man is to me!

I was also blessed by a cardiologist at St. Luke's who came in on his day off to bear witness to me about a devastating accident that had left him in similar shape more than fifteen years earlier. He was broadsided in his car by an ambulance and sustained almost identical injuries to mine. He said it took him weeks to even realize what had happened and many more months of grueling physical therapy. Fifteen years later, he's a practicing cardiologist with no visible signs of his injuries. God is so good to put me in this place with people like him — he wasn't even on my case! This connection was just one more miracle of many.

The day they took out my trach is a poignant memory because that procedure was so unexpectedly painful. I have strange images in my mind of my friend Elizabeth assisting at this procedure, which of course she did not, but that's how I remember it — being propped up in some-thing like a dentist's chair and her leaning over me helping the doctor take out the tube. In reality, Elizabeth *was* there that day and she *was* more interested than most in observing this procedure as she was in nursing school at the time, but she assured me she did not assist in any way. Crazy mish-mash of dreams and real life.

I wanted to talk so badly after that, but was still unable. My throat was horribly sore and raw, and the open wound from the trach needed time to heal. I found myself having little conversations in my head. When I was finally able to get a few words out, my first were uttered through tears and directed at Mike, "I'm sorry. I love you. How are the kids?"

He replied with something like, "The kids need you. You have to fight to get better for them." Despite the fact that I was exhausted and totally terrified of what lay ahead, Mike said just the right thing. Those words fueled the resolve I needed in that moment to power me through. I *had* to fight. Damn it, I was going to fight! I was going to do this!

Some of my fondest memories during this time are of Mike's brother Dave. He had flown in after the initial crisis subsided to relieve Mike, who had been at my side non-stop. Mike was understandably exhausted and needed a break. Dave would sit with me for long stretches of time, and I remember thinking, "Wow! I can't believe he's here. That's really cool!" I love all of Mike's family, but since no one else lives near us, I can't say I was particularly close to Dave, or any of Mike's siblings for that matter. I enjoyed them thoroughly when we got together, but to think that Dave would leave his family to help Mike and to sit with me was amazing. It was a humbling realization, and I was so glad to have him there. Not being able to move or speak made me feel eerily vulnerable, like I was a victim just lying there, and it scared me. I did not want to be left alone, so it was incredibly comforting to have Dave there in Mike's absence. I knew I was in good hands and I felt safe and protected. I never told Mike any of that because I couldn't, but it's as if he just knew. He sensed my fear and he made sure I was never alone.

Having Dave Kern there also resulted in some comical moments. One afternoon, Mike and Dave were trying to figure out what I wanted. It was still very difficult for me to speak, and when I did speak, it was extremely difficult for others to understand me. I was trying to communicate to Dave and Mike that I wanted Chap Stick. My lips were always so dry in the hospital! Imagine, just a couple weeks before, if I had wanted Chap Stick, I would've dug it out of my purse and put it on effortlessly, thrown the tube back where I had found it, and not given it another thought. Now, the simple act of not only putting the Chap Stick on, but telling someone I wanted it, were gargantuan tasks, almost insurmountable hurdles. Mike and Dave diligently tried to decipher what I was gesturing and grunting, but no matter how hard I tried, they weren't getting it. It was like a very bad game of charades.

They would say, "Do you want to be fluffed up? Blink once for yes, twice for no."

Two blinks.

"Do you want another pillow?"

Two blinks.

"OK, are you cold? Do you want a blanket?"

Two blinks.

"Umm...do you need to move?"

Two blinks.

It went on and on, and as my frustration was reaching its peak, Dave said, "We're like Larry, Moe, and Curly here. We're wandering around like the Three Stooges and we have no clue what's going on! Who's on first?"

Well, Mike and Dave absolutely cracked up. They thought the reference to the Three Stooges was so funny. Needless to say, I did not share in their frivolity – I just wanted the Chap Stick!

A mere few minutes after this ridiculous scene played out, one of the nurses came in to check my vitals, and as she was doing so, she started asking me a barrage of questions, like they always did, to assess my cognitive function. They were constantly making sure I knew who I was, who Mike was, where I was, and on and on.

"Do you know who this is?" she inquired, pointing to Mike.

"Moe" was my prompt reply.

The look of concern on her face said it all – she thought I was having another stroke or something. Mike and Dave, of course, were howling. They knew I was joking, and Mike said later that it was another milestone because if I was joking, he knew I was really in there. My sense of humor was intact -- thank goodness, because I was going to need it!

Chapter 7

LONG ROAD

*"Come to Me, all you who are weary and find
life burdensome, and I will refresh you."*

MATTHEW 11:28

ABBY

The ICU was so full of death, it scared me, and even though the medical professionals kept saying that things with my mom "looked good," I could not totally trust that. I kept going back to the day of the accident when they said the very same thing. Clearly, they were wrong then; they could be wrong now. I found myself constantly on edge, like I couldn't allow myself to be too happy or too carefree because what if things took a turn for the worse again? I went from never expecting the worst-case scenario to never anticipating anything *but* the worst-case scenario. Even as I saw my mom making progress, the relief I felt was tempered with the reality that there *was* extensive brain damage, and we still had no idea if her recovery would be partial or full or what that would look like in day-to-day life. I know I should've rejoiced when they moved her from the ICU to the stroke floor, but I just could not shake the pervasive fear that hung over me like a dark cloud. Too many unknowns, too many things that could go wrong, too long a road ahead to start celebrating yet.

TERRI

Being moved to the stroke floor after just two weeks in the ICU was certainly a sign of progress, but I had such a long way to go and I knew it. I literally could not do anything by myself. I couldn't even sit up without being propped with pillows, and one of the first things the nurses wanted me to do was to go to the bathroom. *Really? I can't support my own body weight, but now I'm supposed to get out of bed, walk to the restroom, and do my business using muscles I don't even remember how to use.* Every single thing they wanted me to do was so unbelievably hard and took so much out of me that there were some days when I barely had the will to try.

During one of my bathroom excursions, the nurse supporting me dropped me, and I fell to the floor like a sack of potatoes. I'm five foot, nine and have an athletic build. I am no petite little girl, plus I was pure dead weight. This nurse had no business trying to help me on her own, and it left a definite impression on me. From that moment on, I was terrified of falling and even more terrified of being left alone without Mike. I felt helpless, completely incapable of advocating for myself. The words were there, but I struggled to get them out. The frustration and fear were overwhelming.

MIKE

Looking out Terri's hospital room window, all I could see were giant cranes hoisting enormous piles of beams and roofing materials to the tops of the buildings surrounding us. Inside Terri's hospital room, that scene was mimicked by the gigantic Hoyer lift they used to get Terri up and out of the bed. It was the most inhumane, medieval torture-like contraption I had ever seen, and even worse was the way they would sort of wad Terri up in a blanket to get her up into it. There was nothing pretty or graceful about it, and I know Terri hated it, but she hated being dropped even more.

I made a concerted effort to befriend the numerous medical professionals who cared for Terri. Getting a glimpse into their work was eye-opening, and I do not envy their jobs. After the nurses dropped Terri, I wasn't angry, but I wanted them to remember that she was a real person with real feelings. While she may not have been able to communicate clearly, she was very much alive and deserved to be treated with the utmost respect and dignity. Terri was (and is) a strong woman. She doesn't do "vulnerable." That's what made this all so painful to observe, and the hardest part was that there was not much I could do about any of it to make it better.

TERRI

While on the stroke floor, I underwent an array of assessments. When the speech pathologist came in, I had to pass a swallow test. Check. Then I had to repeat back the five words she said. Check. I had to state my address. Check. When the occupational therapists came in, they worked on my fine motor skills and gave me exercises to try to relax the muscles in my right hand that had been clenched and stiff when I was posturing. While I had sustained damage to both sides of my brain during the strokes, my right side was clearly more affected, which made everything more difficult for me. I wanted to learn to do things left-handed, but they refused to allow it. They said if I was right handed before, I would be right handed again. I had to relearn and they made me work at it even when I didn't want to.

Physical therapy was, by far, the most challenging and the most grueling. Just getting to the "gym" was a workout in and of itself. They had to hoist me up using the harness to get me in the wheelchair. That alone was exhausting, then they would wheel me down to the gym, put me on the mat, and I would just fall over. I had zero trunk support, so that was what I had to work on – just that, just sitting up. I had been a runner, an athlete, and now my entire workout regimen consisted of trying to sit up without pillows supporting me. It was mind boggling and excruciatingly humbling.

All of it was humbling. Having to relearn how to function and accomplish all the daily tasks that two weeks ago I had done so automatically was the hardest thing I have ever done. I remember the first time they brought a tray of food in for me. I had passed the swallow test, which meant I could start to eat solid food. The only problem was that I could not remember how to eat. I knew *what* I needed to do to get the food on the fork and the fork to my mouth, but I couldn't do it, and I guess they just expected me to figure it out because they brought the tray in and just left. *Hello? A little help here?*

Lynn happened to come in right about that time and commented on the fact that I had lunch. I said, "Yeah, but I don't know how to eat it." Talk about pathetic. In a moment of sheer grace, Lynn, trying not to embarrass me, asked if I wanted some help. I nodded. Lynn fed me that day, and again, it just reinforced the enormity of what I could not do and what a long road to recovery I had ahead of me.

MIKE

Physical therapists can come off as tyrants, but I completely understood the method to their madness. They *must* push you as far as you can go, maybe even beyond your limits; otherwise you'll never be motivated to get better. It is only through sheer will that people come back from accidents like Terri's. The temptation to give up is strong. You have to be stronger. Thank God Terri is the strongest person I know because if the tables were turned, I don't know if I could have done it.

I never saw Terri give up. She cried sometimes, and I know she was frustrated, but I never saw her resign or settle, and I certainly never heard her ask the question, "Why me?" I didn't either, but I *did* ask, "What in the heck happened?" I went back to the location of the accident right outside our subdivision time and time again, trying to reconstruct the scene in my mind. I could not wrap my head around how it all transpired. I wanted to understand, to see it, but the more I tried, the more the facts of that fateful day eluded me.

As if she wasn't already dealing with enough, the doctors discovered yet another injury Terri sustained in the accident, an injury that had gone undetected due to the other more serious and complex issues they were dealing with in those first few days. Any time the therapists got Terri to a standing position, she was unable to bear any weight on her right leg and complained of pain. Dismissing it at first, upon further examination, they found considerable damage to her right leg, and when I say, "considerable," I'm not exaggerating. She had a torn MCL, PCL, ACL, and meniscus. That alone would send most people into surgery and rehabilitation for months, and here Terri was dealing with that on top of everything else she had been through. Because these issues were not addressed immediately, the doctors felt like there was no rush to do surgery. Terri wasn't strong enough to handle that at this point, so the short term solution was a very heavy and cumbersome brace. It wasn't a great solution because it made it even harder for Terri to move that leg, but it was the solution we had to work with at the time. It was a setback for sure, but in the big scheme of things, it was a minor one considering where we had been and the road ahead we still had to travel.

TERRI

If I hadn't already realized how pathetic and sad this whole situation was, one of the last things I remember from my five days on the stroke floor certainly drove that point home. They decided I needed a shower, which was certainly accurate because it had been several weeks since my accident – I had had sponge baths, but this would be my first real shower. The thought of warm sudsy water cascading from head to toe *sounded* amazing, but the reality was a far cry from how good I remembered a shower feeling. They stripped me down, put me in a plastic, waterproof wheelchair, and wheeled me in to the shower stall where they proceeded to hose me off like an animal. I was mortified. *Where's my dignity? This is so sad. If anyone could see me, this is so sad and humiliating.*

I do not in any way fault the nurses who were caring for me. They did the absolute best job they could to preserve my dignity – how else can you shower someone who can't even hold themselves up. I get it… but "getting it" does not diminish the sheer degradation I felt that day nor the utter loss of any shred of dignity I had left. I was completely dependent on others to take care of me, and I had to trust that they *would* take care of me. I had to let go, and that was not easy.

As much as I tried to stay positive, sometimes I felt such deep sadness, and sometimes I felt such burning anger. Sometimes I was paralyzed with fear – is this as good as it's ever going to get? – and at other times, I was racked with envy. It was painful to see how everyone else's lives around me remained fairly "normal." They could still go on walks, drive their cars, come and go as they pleased. The world was going on without me, and I was stuck. Quite frankly, I was jealous.

At times, I even allowed myself to venture out a few steps on to the slippery slope of "What if'" and "Why?" What if I had gone a different route that day on my run? What if I had left five minutes earlier? What if I had left five minutes later? Why me? All questions with no real answers, and I knew this line of thinking led me nowhere, but there were days when that's all I *could* think about. I would replay it in my head and imagine different scenarios, all of which involved me walking away unscathed. For a moment, it helped me forget the reality that I was very much affected and changed by what had happened.

If it hadn't been for Mike pushing me, I don't know if I would've had the will power to keep fighting. I am so thankful he loved me enough to be hard on me at times. He told me decidedly one day, "You *have* to sit in the chair more. Every day when I come, you're in the bed. You have to spend less time in the bed and more time in the chair." I knew he was right, but I didn't want to spend more time in the chair --- it was hard, and the bed felt so good. Luckily, Mike knew I needed some nudging and he wasn't afraid to say the hard things I needed to hear.

MIKE

I felt helpless. Utterly helpless to protect and defend the one person I took vows to protect and defend. The Terri I knew was strong, capable, in charge. I knew this must be killing her to be so dependent on everyone else for literally every little thing. All I wanted to do was hug her close and tell her everything was going to be all right…but I couldn't. She was like a fragile egg – I was even afraid to squeeze her hand too tightly for fear of hurting her. And honestly, she was not interested in any affection. She was kind of closed off inside herself. She wasn't able to share with me what was going on in her heart and mind, and I understood. It was too difficult and expended too much energy for her to say much. She saved her energy and words for when she really needed to communicate. It took all she had most days to just get through the little bits and pieces of therapy. That was the hardest part for me. I had lost my confidant. Terri was the person I shared all my thoughts and feelings with, and at this point, that Terri – *my* Terri -- wasn't there.

TERRI

Being surrounded by all the other patients on the stroke floor was overwhelming. It was loud and frustrating, too much stimulus for me at that point. My brain was still healing and it felt like a raw and open wound. Sound and light were painful and confusing. *I don't like it here. I don't want to be here.* That probably explains why I started having vivid dreams of going home. In my dreams, I could walk and get around the house just fine. Why *couldn't* I just go home? In my mind, I knew how to walk, and I knew what I needed to do to function normally. I'll just do what I know I need to do – it seemed so simple.

Of course, it wasn't that simple and I couldn't just walk or function normally – not even close. Even though I understood that my desire to go home was completely irrational, I still felt angry and sad when Mike finally said the words out loud, "Terri, I can't take you home." I knew he couldn't, but I also knew he didn't want to take me home like this. He was trying to have me moved to St. Luke's South because it was much closer to our home, and he felt like the smaller environment there would be more conducive to rehabilitation and recovery.

While that would indeed prove true, I couldn't help but feel annoyed. No one asked *me* what I wanted. Everyone was always putting me here, taking me there, and it was always someone else making the decisions for me. I was a strong, confident, intelligent woman used to running my own show. I know now that I was in no shape to make any substantive decisions about my own care, but at the time, it felt insulting. I just wanted someone to say, "Terri, what do *you* want?" And since that didn't happen, it was difficult to keep up the good fight. I was conflicted between the part of me that knew I had to keep going for my family and the part of me that questioned why any of it mattered anyway. I couldn't see how any of this was ever going to get better. Every night, I held my rosary and prayed. I couldn't remember the right words to the prayers, but it didn't matter. I just prayed that God would give me enough strength to make it through another day.

MIKE

The stroke floor, while a considerable improvement to the ICU, was still the hospital. People were coming in 24/7 to check Terri's vitals, run tests, etc.... It's loud and busy all the time. Despite the fact that Terri was receiving superb care, I realized that this may not be the best place for rehabilitation and recovery. I didn't necessarily want to move her because I felt so secure with Dr. Camarata at the helm, but a transfer to St. Luke's South meant that Terri would be just minutes from our house, and a smaller facility more focused on rehabilitation meant that Terri could focus on getting better.

"Getting better" was something we talked about extensively, but no one was sure at that point what it really looked like. *What would healing mean for Terri?* The doctors and therapists on the stroke floor said that following a brain injury like Terri's, recovery could take up to eighteen months. That seemed to be the magic number – eighteen months. They said that anything not regained after that point was likely lost forever. So, we had eighteen months to get this thing figured out and on the right track. I felt optimistic at that – eighteen months seemed like a long time away, and as I looked around at the other patients on the stroke floor and talked to their families about where they were in the process, I could see that Terri had already made some remarkable strides. Eighteen months was a huge window of time – plenty of time in my mind – to get Terri back.

I was standing just off the curb to the left of the small sign and huge grey light pole. The grass path is only five feet wide and somehow I landed mostly on the grass 35 feet away!- Miracle number one!

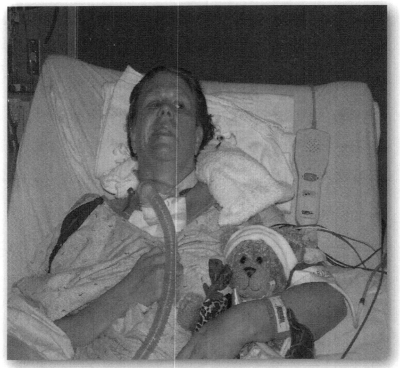

Just waking up to my new reality.

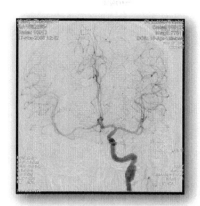
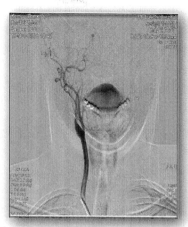

Pictures of my head and neck...the big dark tubes are my carotid arteries-both were dissected with limited blood flow. The big black dots are where the blood clotted and flicked clots to my brain causing strokes...

Another MIRACLE I survived!!!

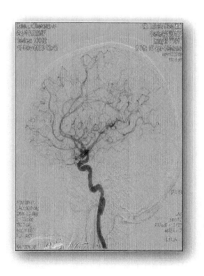
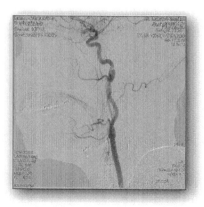

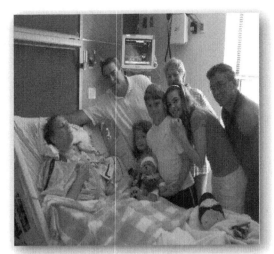

Terri, Mike, Halley, John Milton, Kay, Kaitlyn, and Mike's brother Dave.

Nothing works quite right. It looks like I am pushing
Abby away, when I am really trying to hug her!

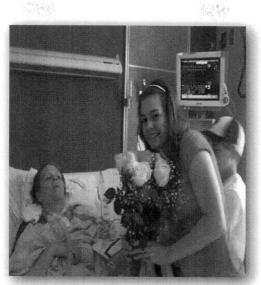

Kaitlyn and John Milton bring light to a dark time.

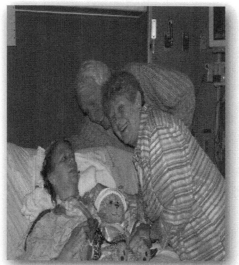

Kay (mom) and Allan (dad) are happy to see me awake.

Tracheotomy tube came out. I am making progress...
now I just need to learn how to talk again.

Moved out of the ICU to the Stroke

Recovery Floor.

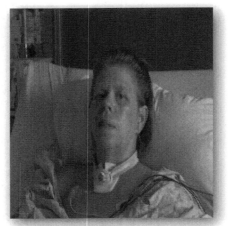

Believe me, I feel much worse than I look!!!!

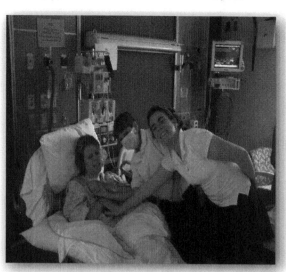

John Milton and Courtney help me sit in a chair with tons of pillows!

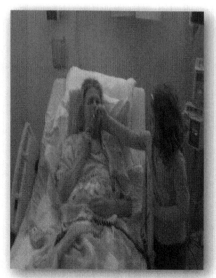

My lips were never chapped when my Little Halley was visiting.

A glimmer of Hope that I can be a Mom again.

Making progress. Tracheotomy wound is healing and on to the Fourth Hospital- St. Luke's South.

My Healing Team:

Courtney, Kaitlyn, Elizabeth (friend), Maggie(friend), and Abby.

Trial visit home. Happy and scared....notice my
fashionable gait belt...easy to grab in case I fall.

Nurses are such a blessing!

Dad not letting go!!!!

First time sharing a bed together in a long time.

Navigating the stairs was terrifying- I must have complete trust.

Back to the hospital for more Rehab!

Dad was my morning meal partner. The last time he fed me was 42 years ago.

Coming home to stay- the ribbons and signs were awesome to see!!

On to outpatient therapy- my new friends (Therapy Team).

First time I felt "normal" in a long time.

My extended family surprised me by coming to Kansas to be with me and......

GIVE THANKS!
Romans 8:28

My Best Friend and Sister-Tracy.

My mom (Kay) kept her promise to me and was received
into the Catholic Church through Baptism.

God may not always answer
Prayers in your time or the
Way you think, but He does answer your PRAYERS.

We are so thankful for God's Mercy-time to give back....

Benefit Walk for Stroke Research.

Back with my Best Friend!

This has been on our bathroom wall for the past eight years...

Chapter 8

NEW PATHWAYS

"So whoever is in Christ is a new creation:
the old things have passed away;
behold new things have come."

2 Corinthians 5:17

TERRI

You'd think I would have been ecstatic to move to St. Luke's South as much as I hated the stroke floor, but it was far more frightening than anything. You'd think I would have been ecstatic to be outside since I had not been outdoors in twenty-one days, but it was far more overwhelming than enjoyable. They wheeled me out in what felt like a rickety wheelchair, strapped it down in the back of what seemed like a very ordinary minivan, and unceremoniously sent me off to the fourth hospital in three weeks. I couldn't even sit upright, so I was slumped over to one side, decked out in a lovely hospital gown, watching the world whiz by outside the window, a world that I barely recognized, a world that hurt my brain to even look at. It was too much stimulus. At a red light, I looked out as Mike pulled up beside the van. We made eye contact. "Isn't this sad?" I questioned him with my eyes. "Why can't I be in your car? Why can't I just go home? Why can't all of this just be different from what it is?"

MIKE

I had tremendous anxiety about this move. I didn't know if it was the right decision, but I knew I had to trust: trust the doctors, my own ability to make clear and good judgments, and most of all, trust the good Lord to continue to provide and protect us as He had done throughout the entire ordeal thus far. I hated seeing Terri wheeled into that van and bolted down so the chair wouldn't slide. I would've loved nothing more than to scoop her up in my arms, put her in my car, and drive her home, but that was not a realistic possibility. Not yet. I had no doubt that at some point, that *would* be the reality, but there was much work to do before that could happen. The doctors said she could be at St. Luke's South for six months, maybe more. We had to hunker down and just concentrate on making progress. When I pulled up next to the van, Terri looked absolutely miserable and forlorn. I didn't know what she was thinking, but in her eyes, I saw such sadness, my heart broke for her. I hoped she knew that I was doing my best for her right now. I hoped she knew how much she was loved, not just by me, but by our children and our entire community as well. I hoped she had a little reserve of physical and spiritual strength left to tackle this next phase of the journey. Actually, I *knew* she did. I just hoped she knew it too.

TERRI

I was greeted at St. Luke's South by Mike and my dad and wheeled into a lovely corner room with big bay windows. The kids had decorated it with inspirational posters and flowers – it felt bright, cheery, and welcoming. My friend Laura brought me a plaque with my favorite scripture verse, Romans 8:28 -- "We know that all things work for good for those who love God who are called according to his purpose." Mike made a sign that still hangs in our house to this day that reads, "Let's move mountains together – God." They even brought some of my things from home, a crucifix and comfy blankets, making it much homier...and more permanent, which was a little unsettling.

Right away, I noticed the "FALL RISK" sign on the door and on my admission bracelet. *Oh my gosh, how embarrassing, I'm a fall risk!* Mike chuckled at my concern, "Terri," he reassuringly soothed me, "*Everyone here is a fall risk!*" I think I still saw myself as I was before, the old me. I couldn't wrap my brain around what had happened and the new me that had emerged.

What I did have to wrap my brain around fairly quickly though was the fact that they were not going to let me lay in bed at this new facility. I had to get up and get dressed every single day, which was an excruciating task at first, and one that I didn't understand. *I'm in the hospital! Why does it matter if I'm dressed? I'm certainly not going anywhere and no one is going to see me. Who cares? I don't want to get dressed!* If I could have, I would have stomped my feet and wrung my hands in an all-out temper tantrum that would have rivaled the world's most ornery two-year-old, but I couldn't, and it took too much energy to fight the inevitable anyway. So, I learned how to get dressed in a wheelchair with a catheter, which was not pretty or graceful by any stretch of the imagination, but something I eventually figured out. In the beginning, just getting dressed was my biggest and greatest accomplishment of each day. I probably should have felt proud, but I had a hard time believing that this was me and an even more difficult time shaking the sense that this was all so very sad.

Everything, and I mean EVERYTHNG, was therapy in this place, from getting dressed to putting on make-up, to brushing my teeth and hair, to eating, to playing card games, and the list could go forever. Nothing came naturally to me anymore. I had to think about each and every movement. All the old neural pathways were damaged, so I had to create new pathways to do all the things I had known before, and the only way to do that was to practice and repeat.

One of the most difficult things I had to master was tying my shoes. Mike was usually there when I was getting dressed and undressed each day to offer his assistance as needed. Even after I mastered the getting dressed thing fairly well, he always tied my shoes. I didn't even try because I would look down and just think, "I have no idea how to even begin to do that." I'll never forget the day when he said that he couldn't help me tie my shoes any longer. I had to learn to do it myself. The nurses told him he had to step back, that the longer he did things for me, the longer it was going to take me to get out of there. Looking at my tennis shoes, it was like my legs weren't even connected to my body – *Were those someone else's shoes?* I didn't remember how to tie my shoes, and no matter how hard I tried, I could not conjure up any framework for this in my brain. It was gone. *OK, here we go, another mountain to move.* It was so hard for Mike to watch me struggle, but he did what they said. He stepped back, and I learned how to tie my shoes – it only took me two days!

With every small victory came a tiny morsel of renewed confidence, strength, and hope. I had lots of cheerleaders urging me on. Unlike the previous hospitals, visiting hours were much more lax, so the kids were able to come and spend longer periods of time with me here, which was therapy in and of itself. John Milton liked to play with the remote control for the bed, and often he would crawl up in bed with me and watch TV. I loved that. The girls came up quite a bit too. We had mini sleepovers where they would do my hair, paint my nails, and fill me in on what was happening in their lives. Halley liked to help feed me, which was always comical because for some reason, they thought that Jell-O was the optimum food for someone who was re-learning hand-eye coordination. Inevitably, the Jell-O ended up everywhere except in my mouth. We always had a good laugh about that. We even had mommy-daughter haircut day because Halley refused to get her hair cut without me, so my parents brought her up to the hospital, and we did it together.

I was also visited frequently by my friends Patti and Lynn who came to pray with me. They were part of a prayer group I belonged to, and since I could not make it to the meetings, they came to me. We had joined forces years before to offer prayers for a friend with colon cancer. Sadly, he lost his battle with cancer, but we stayed together, united in prayer and fellowship. A diverse group from different faith backgrounds, we found strength in our common prayer, strength that carried me through the difficult days of rehab and beyond. To this day, we still gather monthly.

While I loved having the kids there and all the other friends and family who visited, too much stimulus was still hard for me. If the room was full and there were multiple conversations happening concurrently, I couldn't follow. It was too taxing. Mike noticed and started to limit my visitors, which helped, but even trying to follow a single conversation was arduous. It took me longer than before to process what I was hearing. Then, it took me even longer to formulate the words in my brain to respond, not to mention how long it took me to actually speak them aloud. It was frustrating, and just one more thing that was different since the accident.

Physical therapy at St. Luke's South was a much more pleasant experience in many respects than at St. Luke's on the Plaza. For one, it was right down the hall, so getting to the gym was much easier. Second, there were far fewer patients, so it was quieter and less stimulating. This allowed me to focus on my therapy. Sometimes, the kids or my mom would accompany me to PT. The most grueling part was trying to walk, gripping those darn parallel bars while they had me strapped in a gait belt, and trying with all my might to pick one foot up and set it back down. *This used to be so automatic — why is it so hard now?* I would look at people outside my window walking around and think, "Do you know how hard it is to walk? How much effort it takes? No, you don't, and I didn't either, but now I sure do, and you should never take it for granted!" I remember the day I took three whole steps and the kids erupted in cheers. True to form, in my head, I was thinking how utterly sad and pathetic it was that we were celebrating three steps because to me, that was nothing worth celebrating. We'll celebrate when I can walk into my own house and up the stairs. That thought, plus the kids' unrelenting encouragement, urged me on.

Mike's unshakable faith spurred me on as well. He was convinced that God spared me for some very specific reason and that He worked this miracle in my life for my family and others to witness. Even though I often felt weak, sad, and frustrated, something deep down knew he was right. I was a fighter and had to keep fighting. I had to get back to my family, and I had to get better for whatever God had in store for me in the future. I couldn't imagine what that might be, but I knew I wouldn't be of any use unless I was strong again.

In addition to Mike and the kids, I had two very special and frequent visitors while I was rehabbing at South, my father and my parish priest. My dad is a sensitive man. It is hard for him to see anyone suffering, so I know it was especially hard for him to watch me go through this. He didn't spend much time in the ICU or on the stroke floor, but now that I was in more of a rehab setting, it was easier and more comfortable for him to visit. He took it upon himself as his "job" to come every morning for breakfast. I started to make it a point to order things I knew he liked so we could share. This time with him was truly precious. We talked and commented on what we saw outside my big windows, and we took bets on which window washer was going to finish first. This frequently involved considerable joking and laughter. As

I made progress, we played cards together — again, very much a kind of therapy. Considering everything I had forgotten how to do, it was rather curious that I remembered how to play gin, and I was still good! Our brains are crazy things.

Father Ron, my parish pastor, was a friend already before my accident. I volunteered in several capacities at church, so I was often in the parish offices, and he always was so kind to Halley, giving her candy and letting her explore the many hidden "treasures" in his office. Over time, we had built a relationship. He came often to talk and pray with me. He taught me about redemptive suffering. He told me not to let my own suffering go to waste, that I could offer it up — use it — for someone else. My suffering could be my intercession for someone else who needed my prayers, and he knew just who needed it. He asked me to pray for another mother from our parish, a woman who was also at St. Luke's South with colon cancer. I knew who she was, but I didn't really know her. She had a daughter Halley's age who had been in a different kindergarten class that year. I'll never forget Father Ron's request, mostly because I did not receive it well at first. *Pray for someone else? You have got to be kidding me! Here I am, in the hospital — I need prayers. I don't have the energy right now to pray for someone else's healing. I need to pray for my own healing.*

Selfish, I know. I'm not proud of the fact that that was my initial reaction. Father Ron nudged me, "You have a rosary, you can pray," and of course, he was right. I did have my rosary; I went to sleep with it every night. It was my lifeline. I *could* pray for her, and I did, every single day. Unbeknownst to me, Father Ron had asked the other woman to pray for me too. I had no idea at the time, but as I think back, Father Ron certainly knew what he was doing. In his quiet, subtle way, he got each of us out of our heads for a while and gave us each a mission greater than our own painful situations. He made sure that neither my suffering nor hers would be in vain. We united our suffering to one another, offering it up, creating a secret, silent sisterhood that neither one of us even knew about. Sadly, she did not win her battle with cancer, but her daughter is good friends with Halley today, and I have a very special place in my heart for that girl growing up without her mother. Halley could be *that* girl, and I pray that if she were, the other mom would love her like her own the way I love her daughter.

MIKE

When I think about Jesus' forty days in the desert, I can relate. The period of time while Terri was focusing on rehab was a lonely time for me. I was wandering in the desert alone, missing the way things were before, praying a lot, listening intently for the still small voice of God to break through the sometimes-thunderous voice of doubt and fear in my head, and still hoping desperately for a miracle. Terri had to concentrate all her time and energy on her recovery, and so it just followed that everyone and everything else around her fell to the periphery. She was in "rehab mode," and driven to get to that finish line. They didn't even want me to come to Terri's physical therapy, and when she was finished each day, she was completely wiped out. We did spend quite a bit of time together, but even that was a far cry from what I was used to. We weren't engaged in our normal lives anymore shuttling kids here and there, arranging schedules, making plans. I didn't realize how much "space" that occupied in our former conversations, but now that it was removed, what did we really have to talk about? I missed my Terri, and I ached for our old lives back.

The various therapists and nurses who cared for Terri at South were amazing, and one, in particular, made quite an impression on me. Her name was Monica, and she told me one day, "Listen, this can make or break your marriage. I've seen it happen far too many times, and I've been there myself. This is just a heads-up; you've got a long road ahead still."

She was certainly right about the long road, and I'm sure she was also right about the fact that this *could* break my marriage, but I was determined to not let that happen. Terri had been my rock during my time of suffering the year before. There was no way I would be anything less than that for her now. My job was to attend to her needs, to be her coach, her cheerleader, and her advocate. It wasn't about me, and I so valued Monica's witness of faith and friendship at a time when I desperately needed it.

On a lighter note, Monica also gave us a good laugh one day when she asked about the other priest who often visited Terri, Father Gabriel. He was the Associate Pastor at Nativity and he always brought Terri smoothies when he came. In the early days when everything seemed so bleak, he was very distraught and frantically anointed every tube, every bag, and every machine in the ICU room with olive oil he blessed for the emergency occasion. He gave us that oil, and it was not uncommon for me to bless Terri with it, making the sign of the cross on her forehead, and for her to do the same for me. When Father Gabriel visited, he continued his practice of blessing Terri and her various equipment with the oil. Once Monica caught a glimpse of this, she asked, "What's he basting you with?"

After we laughed, we explained, and it turned out that she, too, was Catholic, and asked if she could have some of the blessed oil. No problem, except that we're in a hospital and there's not a lot of appropriate containers laying around, so Monica matter-of-factly grabbed a urine sample cup and poured some of the oil inside. As humorous as that was, it didn't even compare to what happened later in the lunch room when she inadvertently set it down on the counter and got a swift reprimand from her colleagues for leaving her urine samples sitting around!

Levity was good, and it came in many forms, sometimes unexpected, but always welcomed. Every time we shared a laugh, I felt like the old Terri had returned. I knew things would never quite be as they were, and I understood that Terri was becoming a "new" person. As I was trying to adjust to that, I cherished the moments of connection between us, a laugh, a smile, a look – I had to reacquaint myself with *this* Terri, and I was more than willing to get to know this beautiful new woman all over again.

Chapter 9

HOME FRONT

"Let the peace of Christ console your hearts."

COLOSSIANS 3:15

MIKE

Life at home was semi-normal, I guess. Honestly, it's hard to say what "normal" even meant for us anymore. Terri's parents and numerous friends were doing a fantastic job of holding down the fort, so in many ways, I surrendered my parental rights for a while. Even when I was there, which was not often, I deferred to whoever else was in charge that day. I know it was confusing sometimes for the kids as to who they were supposed to listen to or take instructions from, and looking back, I empathize with them. It was a confusing time for all of us. The "state of emergency" had peaked and given way to a sort of plateau. The crisis mode we were all in at the beginning morphed into a weird limbo in which we continued to go through the motions of our normal routines, all the while, our lives were completely altered.

None of us knew what to expect in the coming weeks or months, and although it probably appeared that we were doing just fine, in reality, we were all still teetering on the edge.

This was evidenced one afternoon when Kaitlyn got literally knocked out during a soccer game. She and another player ran right smack into each other and hit the ground hard. I was certain she had a concussion, but she absolutely refused to go the emergency room. She was terrified and there was no way I was getting her to budge from the field unless I promised her we would go home instead. To be honest, I wasn't all too thrilled about going to the ER myself. It was too soon. I didn't know if I could handle it any better than Kaitlyn. Luckily, our family doctor and good friend was willing to make a "house call" that night to check her out, and luckily, it didn't warrant any further medical attention. *Are my kids ever going to be able to step foot into a hospital without being paralyzed by fear? Are any of us ever going to really be able to forget? Will we be able to move on?*

JOHN MILTON

School finally ended, summer arrived, and all I wanted to do was escape the house. I wanted to be with my friends and not think about what had happened to my mom or what was happening to her now in rehab or to the rest of us at home. My grandparents did a great job, and I was very thankful to have them there, but they are not my parents, so it just wasn't the same. They didn't always know or understand how things typically ran in our house or what we considered "normal." I'm sure we were an awful lot to handle. One afternoon, they forgot to pick me up from camp — no big deal — but I couldn't help but think, "There is no way this ever would've happened if my mom was here." My mom was amazing. She handled everything and was always one-step ahead of us, anticipating our needs and managing schedules. No matter how much

I loved my grandparents, they could not replace her, and I missed her. We all did.

KAITLYN

My grandparents certainly provided stability to our household, and I appreciated that. It felt good to have them there. I didn't abdicate my role as "mom" completely though. I don't think I ever have, even though I'm an adult now and out of the house. Part of being the oldest is being the parent. I accepted that, and part of me relished it while part of me was angry about it. I was angry mostly at my dad. I felt like he abandoned us during this time. I understood he needed to be with my mom, but I wanted to be kept in the loop, I wanted to know what was happening, and I wanted him to recognize how much I had stepped up to help out. I had taken on a great deal of responsibility, but I felt that he was still treating me like a child. The stress gradually took its toll on me. I couldn't sleep, I lost weight, and I stopped hanging out with my friends. It was completely self-imposed, but I felt like I *had* to be home. I had to be there.... just in case. *What if something else bad happened or someone needed me?*

Layered on top of the anger, I was also so sad. I missed my mom. I visited her daily, but she was not my mom. You could literally see the wheels turning in her head as she attempted to formulate every word, so being with her was awkward and uncomfortable at this point. A depressing and sobering reality was sneaking up on me – this is as good as she's ever going to get. THIS is it. I know I am a negative person by nature. I expect the worst so that I won't be disappointed. In retrospect, I know that's what I was doing. I was so fearful that my mom might not get better, that I started preparing myself for her to be this way forever. I obviously did not give her substantial credit for being the strong woman she is, and in the weeks and months that followed, all my doom and gloom was erased by her amazing recovery. This was one time I was perfectly happy to be proven wrong.

COURTNEY

Like all little girls, I had grown up believing my mother was perfect. The beautiful, athletic, caring, fun-loving, bright woman I called "mom" never messed up, never misjudged, never got cranky, and never inspired anything but sunshine and rainbows. An important milestone in everyone's life is the moment you start to see your parents as the real people they are, imperfect people with unchecked emotions, unrealistic expectations, bad days, and real struggles just like the rest of us. I reached that milestone when I visited my mom at the hospital that summer. As I saw all the nurses fussing over her, I thought how nice it was that my mom gets to be taken care of for once. It was eye-opening to see that she did not enjoy this one bit. She was always so cranky about them helping her, obviously because she was frustrated and wanted to do things herself, but it showed me a whole new side of my mom. It exposed a more human side because I saw her struggle to do simple tasks. Some days I would laugh with her about those things, and some days I would comfort her when she cried tears of frustration. Despite my anger at the fact the accident had happened, I enjoyed getting to know my mother in this way. It made me feel closer to her and more like an adult in the situation. I loved that she let me help her because it was such a new dynamic between us.

ABBY

I'm not going to lie – this was a rocky time for all of us. Under the best of circumstances, a large family is going to experience tensions from time to time, and we were no exception. The problem during this particular stretch of time was that we were not living under the best of circumstances, so to say that there were tensions would probably be an understatement. It likely didn't appear that way to anyone on the outside looking in, but there were definitely times when it felt like we were falling apart. It was a difficult adjustment to have my mom and dad gone all the time and my grandparents acting as "mom and dad." We were a household of strong personalities, with our own ideas about what we should be allowed to do and how things should run. Conflict was inevitable.

I tried to steer clear of that, but I still struggled to let go of the fear that gripped me. I just could not believe that everything was going to be okay again, so I kept myself guarded to avoid being crushed. That summer, I feel like I lost my naiveté. I had gone along through my perfect little life thinking that nothing could snatch that away from me, but we had experienced something so devastating, that I now knew that things like that – or even worse things – *could* happen. I know this realization occurs to everyone at some point, so I understand it's just part of growing up, but I don't think I was totally ready for it yet. I guess you don't get to pick when you grow up.

That summer was also hard because I didn't really want to hang out with my friends. I didn't have time and I didn't want to leave the house for long periods because what if something else happened? It was difficult to share with my friends what was going on because they couldn't understand and I'm sure they weren't all that interested anyway. Junior high girls typically have other things on their minds. It left me feeling alone and I convinced myself it was just easier to stay home. As a result, I lost some of those friendships permanently.

When you're in the middle of a traumatic situation, it feels like an eternity, but now, in retrospect, I can appreciate that this difficult time was just a blink of the eye in the larger scheme of things. I am so grateful that my grandparents were willing to take us on and make the sacrifices they did to live with and care for us. I don't know how we would've made it without them.

KAY

Allan and I loved being with our grandchildren, but it was an adjustment for all of us. We tried to just help, not change things too terribly much, but it's not easy stepping in to other people's lives and trying to manage as you think they would. And this was a lot to manage – five children with busy schedules and routines, needs and wants, summer break approaching quickly. It was even a struggle for me to get used to cooking for so many people. It had been just Allan and I for a long time. It was a challenge we lovingly welcomed though, and we knew how appreciative Mike was. He never ceased to show us his gratitude.

We had so much help and support from Terri's wonderful friends as well. I don't think we could've done it all by ourselves. As a matter of fact, I *know* we couldn't have. Her friends were angels, taking care of so many details that allowed us to just focus on being with the kids. One day I opened the front door to find a large basket full of gift cards. There were gift cards for everything under the sun – enough to keep us occupied all summer long. Thousands of dollars, I'm sure. This was by far the best gift that Terri's friends could have given us. Keeping five kids busy and happy was not easy, and it was certainly not cheap. This allowed us such freedom to go and do and have fun. It made my heart swell to see how loved my daughter and her family were in this community. Of course, *I* think my daughter is pretty special, but to see that others felt that way as well was truly a blessing.

The kids were so helpful and accommodating. They knew we weren't capable of doing everything exactly the way Terri would do it, and they rolled with the punches. It was hard on them, but they kept much of it to themselves. Kaitlyn and Courtney, especially, held a lot of what they were feeling inside and kept up a brave face. Halley was far more scared by it all than anyone realized. "Normalcy" was our goal. I'm sure we fell short, but we made every effort to keep everyone occupied and happy so that Mike could be with Terri and Terri could get better.

I hadn't forgotten my promise to Terri that I would become a Catholic, and I had every intention of following through with that promise. I began meeting individually with Peggy Shrick, the Director of Adult Faith Formation at Mike and Terri's church. This is not the standard way one prepares to enter the Catholic Church, and Mike and Terri were worried that their pastor, Father Ron, would not make an exception to the rule, but he agreed. Peggy also understood our special circumstances and was more than happy to accommodate me through one on one instruction. The relationship that I developed with Peggy through this process was an unexpected blessing, yet another way I saw God working in all of this. I am a pragmatist and have always believed that things happen for a reason. As this journey unfolded, I knew, without a shadow of a doubt, that God was bringing forth innumerable blessings out of a tragic situation, and that once we got through to the other side of all this, we would be able to see those blessings more clearly and to truly appreciate them.

Chapter 10

MOVING MOUNTAINS

*"Amen, I say to you, if you have faith the
size of a mustard seed, you will say to this
mountain, 'Move from here to there,' and it will
move. Nothing will be impossible for you."*

Matthew 17:20

TERRI

At some point during my rehabilitation at St. Luke's South, things started to shift. I was making progress, and I could see it, even though there were still obstacles. Every night, before I fell asleep, the nurse would give me my two most valued possessions, my rosary and my nurse call button. I considered both of these my lifelines. The rosary was my direct link to God, and my call button was my direct link to everything else. I was still unable to get myself out of bed and to the bathroom, so being able to push a button and get a nurse down to my room in a matter of minutes was crucial. One night, the nurse didn't give me my call button, and it was too far away for me to reach. I came completely unglued, totally panicked, and started yelling, but no one heard me. My voice was still not strong and it was still not easy for me to talk, much less yell. *What am I going to do?* I had to figure something out. I calmed myself down and began to think through the problem. I fumbled around and eventually found my cell phone within reach. I called Mike at home and explained what had happened. He called the nurses' station, and someone came down right away and gave me the call button. Problem solved. In that moment, I felt so helpless and frightened, but I was able to accomplish some rudimentary problem solving. *That* meant progress.

On another evening, Mike was at John Milton's baseball game and called because he wasn't going make it in time to help me get ready for bed like he usually did. I told him that was not a problem — he needed to be "dad" and I didn't need him to be there to help me get undressed and settled in for the night. There were people there to help me do that. On this particular night, it happened to be a male nurse, and Mike was worried I would be uncomfortable, to which I assured him I was totally fine. And I was. I didn't need that much help anyway, and *that* meant progress.

I was starting to walk a little using the walker and my language skills were improving. Speech therapy was not so much about relearning to talk as it was about relearning vocabulary, sentence structure, idiomatic expressions, and word retrieval. I was working on writing right-handed as part of my occupational therapy, and although my handwriting looked completely different than it had before, at least I could write. I composed letters to Mike and all five kids as part of my therapy, letters they all have hanging in their rooms to this day. Those letters are a constant reminder for all of us of how good God is and how much we take for granted. They're also a reminder that I am not the same. Mike noticed right away how different my handwriting looked. It used to be loopy and open, but now it was rigid and closed. It looked like the block printing of a very small child. I think each letter consisted of only a few sentences, a far cry from my pre-accident verbose self. The fact that I *was* different would continue to take some getting used to, by all of us.

Rehabilitation can be a lonely road. I was in my room all day – had all my meals there and much of my therapy. The only time I ventured out was when I went down the hall to PT, but even then, it wasn't an opportunity to socialize because everyone was so focused on what they're doing. I had lots of visitors, but there was a part of me that longed to connect with others who truly got it, who knew what I was going through. That opportunity came one bizarre night when the tornado warning sirens started to wail, well after bedtime. Now, imagine a hospital floor full of "fall risk" patients during a tornado threat – what do you do? The nurses wheeled all our beds out into the hallway away from the windows and left us there because, well, where else were we going to go? As we lay there, one by one, we started introducing ourselves and chatting, "What happened to you?" and "How long have you been here?" and "What stage of recovery are you in?" Instant camaraderie developed as we shared our stories. It was the most social thing I had experienced since the accident, and in a weird way, a really lovely way to pass the storm. I was disappointed when it was all over and they wheeled us back into our separate rooms. For the first time, I had an awareness of these other people struggling right along beside me, and I didn't feel quite so alone.

I took another important step toward my old self when I made a decision – probably the first real decision I had made in many weeks. I decided to call John Milton's school. He had had a rough year for numerous reasons, capped off, of course, by my accident. While I had always tried to advocate for my children, I had never requested certain teachers or special accommodations for them before, but I felt like John Milton needed to have a good year this next school year. If I could do anything to ensure that, I needed to do whatever it took, so I did. I called and requested a specific teacher and that he be placed in a class with one of his good friends with whom he had never been in class before. I know some people cringe when parents do that, and like I said, I had never done anything like that before, but I felt justified and empowered by making that call. It was a small return to some semblance of control, something I had in excess prior to the accident, but very little of, if any, since. Deciding to act and regaining control -- *that* meant more progress.

Mike's sister Julie was in Italy at the time of my accident, but flew directly to Kansas City to see me at St. Luke's South. It meant so much to me that she went to the trouble to come. Julie is Abby's godmother and truly a faith-filled woman. She was incredibly supportive and present to the kids while she was in town, allowing my parents a little bit of a breather. It was a joy to have her here and it made me feel so special.

As I continued to make strides, I began to feel very comfortable at St. Luke's South. I was successful there and it felt safe. Dare I say, I liked it. My brother Trip flew back in to see me in June and brought me ice cream. He wheeled me outside, and we had a lovely visit. I remember thinking that this was really nice and I could just settle in to this place and this way of life and be perfectly satisfied. Thinking back on that now, I am appalled that I felt that way for even a second, but at that time, I was sort of lulled into this acceptance of how things were and relishing the security I felt. Deep down, I knew there was hard work still ahead — enormous mountains to move — and I was fearful that I might not be able to do it. *I had come a long way, but how much further would I be able to go?*

Refusing to let me settle in for too long, my nurses and therapists felt like it was time for me to make a home visit — a kind of trial run to see if I could maneuver in our home and what kinds of adaptations I would need there. After dreaming for weeks about being home, I was actually more scared than excited about the idea. I didn't know what to expect and I was worried that I might not pass muster. It felt like a test, one I wanted to pass with flying colors — *what if I failed?*

When we pulled up, I felt strange — a mixture of relief and dread. The house looked familiar, but different too. It had been so long since I had seen it, there were things I didn't even remember about it. The first thing I noticed was that Mike had a railing and stairs put in from the garage to the door to make it easier for me to get into the house. Once inside, the kids were excited and so happy to see me, but they were also a little stand-offish in a way, watching me, observing what I was going to do next. I felt a little like I was on display. I think that none of us knew how to act — this was not an everyday occurrence.

My therapists were trying to assess how well I could function in our home, so they suggested I get a drink of water. With all eyes on me, I slowly ambled in to the kitchen using my walker, while one of my therapists followed behind holding the gait belt. When I got to the sink, I realized I couldn't hold the glass and turn on the tap because I would have to take my hands off my walker, and I couldn't do that without losing my balance. *All right, first test failed.*

My next task was to try to sit in a chair. For the last month, I had sat only in wheelchairs or on the bed, so this was going to be a monumental event — sitting in a chair. We had a few to choose from, but I clearly picked the wrong one because although I was able to sit down in it, I was completely unable to get back up. I had done everything correctly, just like I had learned in physical therapy, but there was no way I could hoist my body up and out of that thing by myself. Therapists with gait belt in tow to the rescue! *Second test failed.*

They encouraged me to keep trying chairs until I found "the one" that I could sit in and get out of without help. I felt like Goldilocks.... this one's too soft, this one's too big, this one's too little, etc.... I kept going until I found one that was just right.

The third and most daunting challenge was getting up the stairs to the second floor. This was crucial — I *had* to do this, and I was determined. Mike had a second railing put on the stairs so that I could hold on with both hands on either side as I went up, like using a walker. They strapped on the gait belt and I proceeded to make my ascent. It seemed like it took at least an hour — it might *have* actually taken that long, I'm not sure. I know it took me a long time. It was the hardest and most physically demanding thing I had done so far, and I chuckled to myself because the thought occurred to me, *If I go tumbling backward down these stairs, I am literally going to crush the therapist holding the gait belt!* Mike must've been thinking the same thing because he asked if he should install a chair lift for me once I came home for good. My therapists said absolutely not! They were adamant that I would walk again and that I would climb those stairs with ease. When Mike asked, "How do you know that for sure?" they replied with the same confident belief in me they always demonstrated.

"We've been doing this a long time. She's got what it takes. Give it time. She WILL do this!"

When I got to the top, I went to our bedroom and felt such joy. My room! I fell on the bed, and it was amazing! I had been in hospital beds for a month or more, so long that I had forgotten how incredible my own bed felt. I could've stayed there forever! Mike flopped down beside me, and I realized we hadn't been in the same bed for all these weeks. What a good feeling — a brief reminder of things as they once were, and a glimmer of hope for things as they yet could be.

Eventually, they made me get up and walk into our master bathroom. Our shower was rather large with a good-sized door, and a built-in shelf type ledge that I could sit on, so that was good. Mike had rails installed in the shower and near the toilet. *Wow, when did he do all this?* All in all, the bathroom was ready for me to come home.

The visit home was bittersweet in that I loved being in my house and seeing the kids and my parents, but it also made it clear that I wasn't doing as well as I thought I was and that I had much further to go. At St. Luke's South, around other rehab patients, I was making progress and exceeding expectations by leaps and bounds. Star pupil. The reality at home, however, was far different from the reality at the hospital. Going back to the real world would be harder than I thought it would be. I was a long way from "normal," and the visit reaffirmed that I wasn't the old "me" anymore and never would be that same person again. I also felt like I was more work and trouble than anything. I couldn't even get myself a drink of water. What was it going to be like to be home full time and not be able to take care of myself the way I once had? I didn't know if I could do it.

MIKE

I knew once Terri went back to the hospital following the home visit that we were getting close to the point where she would be coming home for good. I was ecstatic at the thought of having her back where she belonged, but I was terrified at the same time. I liken the feeling to how I assume most people feel when they bring their first child home. You're so excited, but the realization hits you that you have to keep this little thing alive, that it is going to take an immense amount of work, that you really have no idea what you're doing, and that you are terribly ill-equipped for all of it. That's how I felt at the prospect of Terri coming home.

The fact that Terri's parents were still there and were willing to stay for as long as we needed them was a huge source of comfort and gave me great peace about bringing her home. Her doctors and therapists were confident in her recovery and reassured me that they wouldn't send her home unless they felt like she could handle it. I knew *she* could handle it – it was me I was worried about! *What if I was unable to help Terri the way she needed? What if something happened?*

The doctors had discovered that Terri had small pseudoaneurysms on each of her carotid arteries – remnants of the damage done to these arteries during the strokes. The arteries would need to be reinforced with stents and coils would need to be inserted into the aneurysms to obliterate them, but all of her doctors agreed that this procedure could wait. She needed more time to heal. I was in no way in favor of Terri going under the knife again anytime soon, but I was fearful that these aneurysms could cause Terri to have further strokes. I had to be vigilant and notice every little thing – if she started acting "off" and I didn't catch it, she could be having another stroke. If it went undetected, there could be more damage, or she could die.

Needless to say, this created a great deal of anxiety for me as the doctors talked more and more about her coming home. I didn't let Terri know this. It was important to her that I was in control and that I had a game plan, so I let her think that was true even though it was a complete lie.

Meanwhile, I had returned to work. I wish I could say this was a welcome change of pace, but from the moment I walked back into my office, all hell broke loose. My division of the company I worked for was being sold – *welcome back!* My job for the next six months or so would entail extensive travel, at the end of which time, I may or may not still have my job. Prior to Terri's accident, this news would have sent me spiraling into a frenzy of panicked planning. I would have tried to control the situation first through stewing and worrying about it, then by creating not only a Plan B, but also a Plan C, D, E, F, and G. The accident had changed Terri, and it had changed me too. Rather than fret, I handed it all over to God. I had a new relationship with Christ. He was in control of my life. He always had been; I just fought it sometimes. I was now able to surrender that control fully into His hands. Look at what we had already been through! I had no reason to doubt that God was holding me in the palm of His hand and that everything would work out in the end.

As Father's Day neared, we made the final preparations for Terri to come home. It had only been a month and a half since the accident. Terri had made a remarkably speedy recovery, far exceeding the doctors' expectations. It was hard to believe that she was going to be home, and although I wasn't sure what this next leg of the race would look like, I had every confidence that she would keep "running" at breakneck speed to reach the finish line. I prayed I had the stamina to keep up. I knew there would be more mountains that needed moving, so I better get ready.

Chapter 11

HOMECOMING

*"Not only that, but we even boast of our afflictions,
knowing that affliction produces endurance,
and endurance, proven character, and proven
character, hope, and hope does not disappoint..."*

ROMANS 5:3-5A

TERRI

As much as I had dreamed about home, the reality of actually going home was terrifying, and as the big day approached, I grew more and more nervous. I had grown quite comfortable in my spacious, window-filled room at St. Luke's South, and I knew from my brief day visit home how horribly unready I was for reentry into the real world. I felt some comfort at the thought that my parents would still be there, and I would be going to physical therapy as an outpatient five days a week, eight hours a day. I also felt great joy at the thought that I would be able to hug Mike and the kids any time I wanted. I knew "normal" was still a long way off, but going home was an important step on the road to the full recovery everyone had been praying for.

My goal to return home was Father's Day – June 15. I beat that by two days, so on Friday, June 13, just forty-six days after the accident, we loaded up all the things I had accumulated at the hospital into our van. The outside world was still a lot for my brain to handle, and I had only been in a car twice since my accident, so driving the short distance home was, in and of itself, cognitive overload. Entering our subdivision, the sea of yellow ribbons on all the trees and the giant "Welcome Home Terri" sign overwhelmed me. All I could do was take it all in quietly and slowly.

Once inside, I thought, "Now what do I do?" I didn't start outpatient rehab until Monday – three days away – I could not imagine how I would fill the entire weekend or what I was supposed to do or be anymore. Halley just sat on the floor and looked up at me with expectant eyes. I didn't know if she was waiting to see what I would do, or if she was scared, or if she was holding back from tackling me in a big bear hug. I couldn't tell. It was hard for me to read people and harder still for me to connect – even with my own children!

That was the most frustrating part. I wanted desperately to engage with them, to understand what they were talking about and what was happening, but it was all just too much. In many ways, coming home for me, was very disappointing as it reminded me of how far I fell short of anything remotely close to normal. I imagine it was incredibly disappointing for the kids as well. When you think of someone coming home from the hospital, you think they're better, they're healed. I wasn't better, at least not entirely, and I certainly wasn't the same. I wasn't the "mom" they remembered. *Would I ever be?* No one knew yet at that point.

HALLEY

When you're little, time moves at a different pace. I know now that my mom was only in the hospital for six weeks or so, but at six years old, it felt like an eternity. I got so used to her being away that it felt normal to go through the day without her. When she came home, it felt strange to have her there, and I felt awkward around her. I didn't know how to act, and I wasn't sure what to expect. The great thing about being six, though, was that I was able to adapt pretty quickly. By that first night, it already felt "right" to have her home. I remember sitting around the dinner table and feeling like we were a family again, like that was how it was supposed to be. It felt great.

MIKE

I did a terrible job of preparing the kids for Terri's return home. The "mom" that showed up on June 13 was not the same "mom" they had known prior to April 28. On some level, they already knew that, but I think the extent of what Terri still could not do was far more reaching than they understood. When they visited her at St. Luke's South, they saw her happy and making progress. They did "fun" things with her there, and their visits didn't last too terribly long. They didn't see her struggle to function from moment to moment all day long. They didn't see how painstaking it was for her to do the things she once did with effortless ease. Yes, Terri got a second chance at life, but at this point, it was in a diminished body. Her life was but a semblance of what it once was. I am sure they were shocked as this reality quickly became apparent.

COURTNEY

When my mom came home, I knew intellectually that we weren't out of the woods, but my heart just wanted to pretend she was the same and that our family would be back to the way it was. That dream didn't last long because I could see almost immediately how different she was in our own home. Seeing her struggle to eat and walk in the hospital was acceptable in a way. It made sense; I could wrap my brain around it. She had suffered a severe head trauma and she was in the hospital. I expected her to be struggling to relearn how to do all the things she had done before, but seeing that play out in our house made me realize that nothing would be the same again.

JOHN MILTON

I was so thankful to have my mom home, but she was definitely different. She was extremely emotional, crying all the time, and once she started going to rehab, she was hardly home. Even when she was there, in many ways, she wasn't all there, and I could tell she was struggling with daily tasks even though she did an excellent job of compensating and hiding from us how truly difficult things were for her. In my opinion, she handled her setbacks with the utmost grace. We had relied on her for literally everything before the accident, and now, because we had had to learn to rely on ourselves more, we needed her less. In the end, that was a good thing, but it was weird to have her home but not depend on her for everything.

It was hard not to feel sorry for her. She had been an incredible athlete before, running almost every day and playing tennis when she could, but now she struggled even to walk from one room to the other. It was difficult to see her stumble around physically, but even more difficult to watch her struggle with short-term memory and mental tasks. It was so unlike her. That being said, I knew she was still the same kind-hearted person that she was before the accident, which is the most important thing.

MIKE

As for me, I felt like I had failed, failed to protect Terri from being hit by that car. I know that makes no sense. I wasn't there, and even if I was, I am not sure I could have done anything to prevent it from happening, but in my mind, I had failed. Since I failed, I felt an even greater sense of responsibility to make sure she never got hurt again. To that end, I tried to put a bubble around Terri as much as possible. The blood thinners made her bruise easily. Every time she barely bumped her arm or leg, she would end up with a big, nasty, bluish-yellow reminder. She also had to be extremely careful because if she cut herself, she could bleed out. I warned the kids about being extra careful around her and I probably did too much at times instead of allowing her to do things by herself. It was a tenuous balance between protecting her and letting her be independent. It's like when the kids were little. Sometimes, we had to step back and let them learn through experience, even if that involved pain sometimes. That is how I felt with Terri — as if she was the little girl and I was the parent trying to shield her from experiencing any more pain. Surely she had already had enough.

TERRI

On Father's Day, we all went to Mass — the first time I had been anywhere but the hospital or home. I wanted to go, but it was an incredibly difficult thing to do. First of all, getting ready to go *anywhere* was a challenge because I still couldn't walk without the walker and assistance and I certainly couldn't shower or dress without a considerable amount of help. Mike had shower duty and helped me get dressed and down the stairs. I had to go in the wheelchair, and although I knew I needed it, I didn't want to "stick out" or call attention to myself. I realize how ridiculous that sounds now because there is no way I could not have called attention to myself. Our church community had been such a support system for us that, of course, people were going to not only notice me, but come running with hugs and well wishes. I was a total mess. I was overwhelmed and unable to talk to anyone without blubbering like a baby. We sat in our usual pew, right up in the front, which only intensified my perception that all eyes were on me. I wanted so badly to walk to communion, and even though I could have done it, I moved so slowly, I would've held up the rest of the line. I really *would* have made a spectacle of myself!

The fact that I could walk, but not quickly, presented some problems at home, specifically, at night when I needed to use the restroom. I had been catheterized so long, that I was still relearning what it felt like to "have to go," so once I realized the urge, I didn't have much time. I wasn't able to get up quickly enough to get there, plus I really couldn't walk at all without my big, heavy knee brace, and there was absolutely no way I could get that monster on in a speedy fashion in the middle of the night in a groggy state. The initial solution was a portable toilet right beside the bed. Not glamorous, but very practical. Over time, as I was able to walk better and the portable toilet was no longer necessary, another problem surfaced. My "side" of the bed was the farthest from the bathroom. It doesn't sound like a big deal, and honestly, the real problem was Mike. He could not sleep on the opposite side of the bed. After we switched sides, I would often wake to find his head at the foot of the bed. When I would ask what in the world he was doing, he explained that it was the only way he could sleep. In an attempt to remedy this for him, we flipped our entire room! We put the bed against the facing wall and moved the dressers so the room was oriented in the opposite direction. Problem solved. We must like it because it's still that way to this day.

ABBY

I felt a range of different emotions. I was overjoyed to have my mother home and ecstatic to resume our normal routine of seeing her every day again. I loved showing her the different adaptations to our house. I also liked running around the house to get her things and hold her steady while she tried to balance on her walker. I felt so helpless while she was in the hospital, but this was my chance to actually do something for her now. Even though I was relieved to finally have her home, there was still that part of me that was waiting for everything to go wrong again. I was terrified of being woken up in the middle of the night to be told "things are going south." I lived with that fear hanging over my head for a long time. The unthinkable had happened once. I was terrified of having to go through it again.

It was a long time before my mom resumed her full responsibilities as a mother. During her hospitalization, the main concern was keeping her alive and getting her through recovery. Once she was home, I started to realize how much I needed and wanted my mom to be my mom again. I realized how much I missed her being at my soccer games, picking me up from school, and being the one to give me advice. Even though it was a long time before she returned to these roles, she remained my biggest inspiration. Even if she saw herself as wounded, I saw her as the picture of faith.

TERRI

My new "job" at the Rehab Institute, just four miles from our house, gave me a sense of purpose and accomplishment. It gave shape and structure to my days, and eventually, a sense of belonging and community. Our daily routine started with Mike showering me, which was no easy task. In addition to my bum knee, I still had a feeding tube that had to be cleaned and flushed out daily, and even after it was removed, the wound had to be meticulously cared for for quite some time. Once dressed and ready, he would help me down the stairs. I never went back up during the day until it was time for bed. If I needed to nap, I would nap in my parents' makeshift bedroom downstairs. If I needed something, someone else would have to retrieve it. It was simply too difficult to go up and down for me to have to do it more than twice a day. Mike would then head off to work and I would eat breakfast with my parents. Lynn arranged a carpool schedule for me, so someone would pick me up for rehab at nine o'clock and someone else would drive me home at four.

I took it seriously and viewed it as my job. My days consisted of speech, occupational, and physical therapies, more of what I had been doing in the hospital, but instead of feeling isolated, I was constantly surrounded by other people just like me doing the same therapy, trying to make the same progress on the road back toward normal. I quickly made friendships there. I fit in there. We were all in the same boat and we "got each other." No matter how much other people loved us, no one else can understand unless they've walked that road, so the other patients at the Rehab Institute became my friends and my family for a time.

I liked being at rehab. Being home was hard. I felt like a guest in my own house and an observer, not a participant, in my own life. I napped when I got home from rehab because I was thoroughly exhausted, ate dinner, and usually went to bed by seven or eight o'clock. I had no energy to show affection toward my family at all and no interest or ability to do anything other than just get through the day. I was there, but not really. I even thought at one point that I should just stay at the rehab hospital. Reflecting on that now, it breaks my heart that I felt that way. I would never have preferred to be without my family if I had been thinking clearly.

MIKE

Terri was a different person, no doubt about that. That meant that I had to change too. I had to adapt and readjust my expectations. We had to get to know each other all over again. This was something I was eager to get started with, but it wasn't necessarily something Terri was interested in or even able to do at this point. She had to commit everything inside her to the work of rehab, and quite frankly, there was no energy left for us. There really was no "us" during this time, and while I understood, it was hurtful to see her making friends at the Rehab Institute. It was even more hurtful when she suggested she should just stay there. I wanted her to *want* to be home with us, to *want* to reacquaint herself with me, to *want* my friendship. *Why did she need other friends when she had me?*

The kids were dealing with all of this in their own ways. They seemed "normal" at times, and at others, it was clear that they were all carrying their own heavy burdens. Kaitlyn was in a transition time in her life, looking to college and getting ready to begin her senior year in high school. I know it all took the heaviest toll on her. This was supposed to be *her* time, but instead, she was busy trying to be everyone's "mom" and holding it all together. Courtney, too, kept most of what she was dealing with inside. She understands things deeply but didn't talk about it much. Abby was the most expressive of them all, which was good because I always knew where I stood with her. John Milton is a man of few words, so I worried about him — and still do. Halley was just joy. At six, she was just happy to have her mommy home, and in her world, everything was back to normal because mom was back where she belonged. Kay and Allan were still doing much of the parenting, and since I was gone quite a bit, it was difficult for me to know when to step in. I often deferred to their judgments and decisions when the kids were arguing about something, which I realize, in retrospect, created an ever-widening gulf between the children and me.

TERRI

Catholics are criticized sometimes for our reliance on rote, memorized prayers, but I have to say that as I battled through this difficult time, the rote prayers of my childhood are what saved me. I had no mental capacity to formulate a conversation with God, so all I had were the memorized words of the "Our Father" and the "Hail Mary." I was so thankful that those words were in there and that I was able to retrieve them and use them. As I healed, I started to have more conversational prayer with God like I had done before, but those old standbys are so dear to me. The words said what I was unable to say, and I felt such comfort being able to pray, even if it was rote.

MIKE

I was praying too, non-stop. My favorite was part of a prayer written by St. Francis De Sales in the late 1500's. It held a prominent place on my mirror during that summer, and I prayed it daily:

> *Do not fear what may happen tomorrow;*
> *The same everlasting Father who cares for you today*
> *will take care of you then and everyday.*
> *He will either shield you from suffering,*
> *or will give you unfailing strength to bear it.*
> *Be at peace, and put aside all anxious thoughts and imagination.*
> *Amen.*

It's funny to think that a man living half a millennium ago in France could capture with such perfection exactly what my soul longed to believe. It was as if that prayer had been written just for me.

It was hard not to fear what may happen tomorrow. I *did* worry about the future — would Terri recover to the extent that she would be able to be independent? Would our family regain any sense of normalcy? Would we ever be the same again? Despite all those questions, I knew God could get us through whatever was in store. He had already brought us so far. I had no reason *not* to trust that if more suffering lie ahead, He would equip us with the strength to handle it.

TERRI

My sister Tracy came back in late June to relieve my parents and give them time to return to Utah to take care of some of their own business. It was so good to see her. I knew she had been there in the days immediately following my accident, but I didn't remember, so getting to spend time with her while I was conscious was wonderful. During her visit, she took me to have the feeding tube removed, and it was quite the experience. I was no longer using it for nutrition purposes, but my doctors were hesitant to remove it because I was still on the blood thinners. They wanted to avoid doing much of anything for now for fear that I would lose too much blood, and in their opinion, there was no danger in the feeding tube just staying put. I am sure there was no danger in it staying put, but it was unbelievably inconvenient and cumbersome to deal with. It made the already difficult task of walking and maneuvering that much more difficult because it was long and would get tangled in my clothes and in my brace. Honestly, it was an annoyance I didn't need, and I wanted to have it removed.

A doctor from our church with whom we had become friends agreed to remove the tube for me in his office. While part of me was dreading yet one more doctor appointment, the other part of me was thrilled at the prospect of being untethered, so Tracy and I headed in thinking the procedure would be no big deal, but I was wrong. There was just as much tubing inside my body, or maybe more, than there was hanging on the outside, and as he began to pull, I felt an unexpected and unbearable pain. I squeezed Tracy's hand as hard as I could to keep from screaming. I realize I had been through the ringer, but I couldn't believe how much this simple procedure hurt! I was thankful when it was finally over, but I had to continue to care for the wound site very carefully until it healed. Just one more thing to have to think about and one more thing for someone else to have to help me do.

Since coming home, I experienced countless reminders that things weren't as they should be, not as I had planned them to be, and certainly not how I *wanted* them to be. This was particularly true as July 2, our twentieth wedding anniversary, rolled around. Mike and I had talked back in the spring about going on a pilgrimage to celebrate, either to Rome or perhaps even to the Holy Land. It was something we had dreamed of for many years and something that would have been extremely meaningful for both of us. Those plans were abandoned after my accident, and to be honest, I had almost forgotten, but as our anniversary approached, the distant memory of those plans and that dream was yet one more "thing" changed, altered, gone.

I tended to fixate on the loss — what once was that was no longer. I couldn't help but think, "We could've been in Rome.... we should be in Rome....we'll never be able to go to Rome." Mike was much better at fixating on the blessings. He gave me a card that year that read, "You wanted to give me Italy for our 20th anniversary, but instead you gave me YOU!" It was bittersweet for me — I was overwhelmed at times with thanksgiving that I was alive, and other times, I was overwhelmed with despair at what I could no longer do and how that affected the people around me whom I loved. Lucky in a way, our anniversary usually ends up being a family affair since it falls so close to the Fourth of July, and that year was no exception. It ended up getting lost in the shuffle, which in many ways, was a blessing in and of itself.

MIKE

This was not how the summer of 2008 was supposed to go. Ironically, in October of 2007, we had purchased a lake house in Mound City, KS, a little over an hour's drive straight south of Kansas City. It had been our dream to have a little place for our family to get away and spend time together, an escape from the hectic pace of our daily routines. We had finally made it happen, and the plan was that this summer we would spend time there fixing up the house and enjoying the water. I had even bought a boat earlier in the spring. Kaitlyn would be going off to college in another year, and the rest would soon follow. We were looking forward to making this a memorable summer before everyone started going in different directions.

Obviously, that plan changed, and "our" dream of owning a lake home quickly became my dream alone. Needless to say, Terri was occupied, so I went ahead with the original plan as much as possible, making quick trips down to the house to decorate it and get it ready. I did a terrible job – the place looked like a bachelor pad, but at least it was livable. We decided that over the Fourth of July, it would be a great idea for all of us – Terri included – to spend the weekend at our new place. We thought a little change of scenery would be refreshing for everyone.

I love the water. I find it calming and rejuvenating. Terri had always loved it too, but it became apparent almost immediately that the new Terri did not enjoy life near the water at all, and for good reasons. First, the house is small and there are steps everywhere. It was difficult for her to maneuver around and impossible for her to climb the steep steps to the master bedroom loft. She slept in the bunkroom with the kids. Secondly, she was still unstable on dry land – imagine trying to stand on a rocking dock or stepping into a boat. Bad idea. I should have foreseen how uncomfortable this would have been for her, but I was so excited to have the family all together and to "live the dream" that I did not anticipate the difficulties of this situation well at all.

Terri is a trooper and a darn good actress, so she put on a brave face, smiled and laughed, and tried very hard not to let the kids see how frustrated and upset she was. But I knew. And I knew this was no longer something we could share. It was my thing now, not hers. Considering all that we had been through, I knew it was not a big deal, and in the years since, the house has honestly become more of a pain to upkeep than anything, but in the moment it felt like one more wedge between us, one more step away from how things used to be, and one more step toward an unknown future.

Chapter 12

ALL FOR GOOD

"We know that all things work for good for those who love God, who are called according to his purpose."

ROMANS 8:28

TERRI

The weekend at the lake was hard. Again, I felt like an observer. I couldn't do all the things that everyone else could do, and honestly, I didn't even want to. Where I was once confident and sure-footed, I was now fearful and tentative. I couldn't even trust my own body to do what I thought it could or should be able to do. I was already having a difficult time controlling my emotions, so adding this layer of frustration and stress to the mix rendered me a heaping mess.

Something had to change. I had to try harder to embrace life as it was rather than grieve the loss of what had been. I had to regain some control over what I *could* control and let go of what I could not. I had to try harder to be thankful. I had so much to be thankful for. I had been spared! I was alive! I would be able to savor many years with my husband and children. I had an amazing husband who had done nothing but care for me for months. I had amazing parents who put their lives on hold to care for my children. I had wonderful children who filled my life with abundant light and joy. And I had remarkable friends who continued to pour out their love and support long after I was home.

Although there were still numerous struggles, the second half of the summer marked a shift for me in my attitude and perspective. I continued to make progress, walking with a cane instead of the walker, "graduating" to a smaller knee brace, and finally mastering the art of showering myself. "Mastering" may be too strong a word, but I was learning. At rehab, I found my voice, advocating more for what I needed and wanted to work on. I asked one day, "What if I fall? How do I get back up?" Valid question. So, my therapist placed me on the ground, and I learned how to get myself back up. I also had computer access there, so I was able to log on to the Caring Bridge website and post updates about my progress. I liked being able to do that myself. Much of the Caring Bridge journal had been posted by other people, so now that I was capable of recording myself, I was able to say thank you to the hundreds of people who had been following my story and praying for me. My accident helped me to see that relationships are all that really matter, and it left me far more empathetic toward the suffering of others. I hoped that my story might inspire someone else struggling to persevere through their suffering, or perhaps it might ignite the faith of someone struggling to believe. I remembered what Father Ron had said, "Don't let your suffering be in vain."

I kept pushing forward. Toward the end of July, my dear friend Julie from Wisconsin came to visit while my parents again headed home to Utah for a little break. I had known Julie for twenty years. Our husbands worked together, so we met through them, but over the years had developed a strong friendship all our own. We had traveled extensively with them, and even though they lived in Wisconsin, we had kept in close touch. During the past two decades, Julie and I had had numerous conversations about God, religion, faith, and prayer. Because she was not particularly religious, she questioned me as to why I prayed and why I felt like my relationship with God was so crucial to my life. We had open, honest discourses, and although we disagreed, I always loved engaging in these conversations with her.

During her visit that summer, she dropped a bombshell on me – a big, beautiful, bombshell. The day her husband called her at work to tell her about my accident, she began talking to God. In fact, she wrote me a letter titled, "The Day I Started Talking to God," and in it, she recorded the words of that first, desperate prayer:

> Dear God,
>
> You must've been pretty busy in Iraq watching over our soldiers at 9:08 AM, but Terri needs your full attention back in Kansas City. Please hurry and get there. She is in an ER room with Mike. Please hurry, she needs you. Come on God, my dear friend believes in you completely and deeply. She isn't like me in that I would prefer some DNA evidence before I totally commit to you. She is one of your most faithful children and she needs you to give her strength. Not just a little strength, but full on Superman strong strength. Send all the angels if you can't make it. Please protect my friend. She is totally worth it!
> Amen.

She told me that that very day, she bought a prayer journal and had been praying and journaling ever since! She also told me that she and her husband "Bear" had driven to Kansas City to see me while I was in the ICU. Of course, I didn't remember this at all, but I was so moved that she would've made that long trek just to sit by my bedside. She said she *needed* to be there with me, felt like God was drawing her there. For someone who had not previously been in tune with her inner voice or any sense of the Divine, this was monumental. She and Bear literally dropped everything, even left their children home alone, to get to us. Julie knew I needed her and Mike needed Bear. Apparently, she held my hand, whispered in my ear to stay strong, and read to me from a book she had recently purchased called, *God's Promises to Women*. According to Julie, my accident sparked her belief in the power of God. *WOW!* I was humbled that God could use me to bring his precious daughter Julie back to Him. I guess Father Ron was right again – my suffering had not been in vain.

KAITLYN

As I watched my mom that summer and into the fall, I was blown away. She was working so hard and recovering so quickly – it was almost unfathomable that it had only been a few months since the accident. True to who she was before, everything she did was for others. I saw her relentlessly rehabbing – for us. She fought to get better – for us. She withstood pain and humiliation – for us. I am sure it would've been so much easier for her to give up at times, but she never gave in to that temptation.

Unlike her former self, this new version of my mom had no filter, which resulted in some equally shocking and hilarious moments as she would spout off whatever she was thinking – inappropriate or not. This was such a departure from the old Terri, who was mannered to a fault and never uttered a cuss word aloud, at least not in front of us, kids. It was ironic at times to think how we had switched roles – *we* had to be the ones correcting *her*, gently explaining why she couldn't say this or that, just like she had done for us. My mom is such a humble, self-less person that she took our correction well and joined in our laughter at her sometimes off-color remarks.

She was still my mom, though, and it was hard for me to relinquish the parenting role I had taken on. It was also hard for me not to be a little bit self-centered as the school year neared. It was my senior year. I had so much to look forward to and plan for. This was an important time in my life, and although I completely understood that the focus could not and should not be on me, part of me still wanted it to be. The other thing that troubled me was that my family was acting like everything was back to normal, as if the last few months had never even happened. It did happen! And I wanted to talk about it. I needed to talk about it, to process it, to wrap my seventeen-year-old head around it. Instead, there was a push to just "move on," but I wasn't ready to do that yet. I needed time, but there was none. Life kept moving and I had to run to catch up, leaving some deep wounds unhealed inside of me that would fester for years and eventually explode to the surface.

MIKE

Terri had a follow up appointment with Dr. Camarata at the end of July to assess the status of her carotid arteries. He was going to perform a CT angiogram (CTA) to determine the extent of healing that had hope-fully taken place. If the arteries were not healing satisfactorily, Terri would need to have stents put in, which would mean more surgical procedures and time in the hospital. I hoped and prayed she didn't need them.

I took Terri to the appointment at St. Luke's on the Plaza. It was the first time we had been back there, and as I anticipated, it proved extremely difficult, especially for me. Terri did not have much, if any, memory of her time at St. Luke's, but I remembered every single detail. We ended up in the same waiting room where our family and friends had prayed the Rosary during Terri's arteriogram, the night no one thought she would survive. Here we were, three months later. It was surreal, it was overwhelming, and it was humbling. Throughout this journey, we had encountered many families in the various hospitals who were going through similar trials. Some of their stories didn't end well. *Why did ours? Why did Terri survive? Why was her recovery going so well?* She always quotes a verse from Romans that says that God can use all things for good. I had to believe that was true. This would be used for good – it already had been – and I continued to pray that God would keep using us and our story and that there was still more good to come from the suffering we had endured.

The CTA revealed that Terri's arteries were healing nicely. As it turned out later, she would end up needing stents, but that was several months away. For now, we got the good news that all was well, Terri could come off the blood thinners, and she should keep doing what she was doing because whatever it was, it was working.

TERRI

We had already planned a trip for all of us to my parents' cabin in Island Park, Idaho at the beginning of August. Mike was busy back at work, and obviously, I was not in any condition to travel, but we thought it would be a great idea for the kids and my parents to go ahead. Courtney decided to stay with me, for which I was so thankful, but we put the other four children on a plane with my parents and waved good-bye. It was hard to send them off. I valued every moment of time with them after being away from them for so long, but I was happy they were going to get to have a little more fun before school started and a little bit of normalcy to cap off their summer.

The one on one time with Courtney was a blessing. With five children, you have to be purposeful about planning that kind of time or it just doesn't happen. It was a rare treat to get to spend my days with her. We watched movies, went shopping and out to lunch, and even went to work out at the gym. Of course, all of this was hampered by the fact that neither one of us could drive. Thank goodness for good friends who were so accustomed to chauffeuring children around all day that they didn't mind adding us to the mix.

Courtney helped me do the many things I still couldn't quite do myself, like getting dressed and cleaning my feeding tube site. It was quite the role reversal. In February before my accident, she had broken her shoulder and needed help doing everything. Just five months ago, I was dressing her, and now here she was, doing the same for me.

The week after the kids and my parents returned, we all participated in the Stroke Stroll and Run to help raise money and awareness for stroke victims. Many of our neighbors, fellow parishioners, and friends joined us, making it a beautiful day to offer thanksgiving and glory to God for all He had done. As I held Mike's hand and slowly walked the single mile, I told myself to remember this struggle in my life as it brought me that much closer to my Lord and Savior. At church that day, we had sung, "Be Not Afraid." I *had* been afraid – terribly afraid – but I had also known the comforting presence of God right beside me through the entire ordeal. There were still plenty of difficulties down the road and many things I was still struggling with, but God had a plan for my life. I believed it with my whole being and I desired to embrace that plan, whatever it might be. Prayer is powerful, God is mighty, and with Him, all things are possible. I was overcome that day with gratitude and joy for ALL that had been – the good, the bad, and the ugly. It was ALL part of the plan.

Two days later, we said good-bye to my parents as they headed home to Utah in a rented Suburban loaded down with all the things they had accumulated during their three-month stay. I was sad to see them go, but also ready. It was time for Mike and me to step back into our roles as parents and authority figures. It was time to reclaim my house and my way of doing things. It was time for our family to settle back in to school, work, and whatever the next season might hold in store for us.

The satellite branch of the Rehab Institute near our house closed, so for the rest of August, I did outpatient therapy back at St. Luke's South a couple days a week. They sent me home after that with all sorts of exercises and therapies to do on my own, so while the kids were in school, I worked at continuing to improve my fine motor skills and gradually took on more of the household roles I held before the accident.

I had made a quick recovery to be sure, but the doctors reminded me to be patient and said that the last twenty percent or so of recovery may come more slowly than the first eighty percent had. I was walking better, but I always had to have shoes on, even in the house, and I had to be very purposeful about where I was heading. I had to anticipate obstacles and plan around them before I even took the first steps to get where I was going. That initial fall way back on the stroke floor when the nurse dropped me had frightened me and still plagued my thoughts at every move.

Over time, I became more and more proficient at functioning in our own house, but the outside world was a different story. I wished I could wear a sign that read, "Brain injury survivor – gimme a break." Physically, on the outside, I looked fine. If you didn't know what had happened or didn't know me before, I appeared "normal," but I wasn't. On the inside, my brain still felt jumbled. I couldn't multi-task to save my life or remember a series of directions. At Back to School Night, I was overwhelmed by the noise and the crowds. I was trying to find classrooms, navigate unfamiliar hallways and large groups of people, take notes while the teachers explained their expectations and procedures, and I couldn't do it. *Why can't I do this? I've done it for years and years. Why is it so hard?* I thought I should be able to do things that I couldn't, and that realization was always frustrating. Everywhere I went and everything I did reminded me of how profoundly the accident had impacted me.

The biggest hurdle still looming ahead was driving. Our friends and neighbors had been incredibly helpful, and I knew that I could call any number of people any time and ask for a ride anywhere I needed to go, but I longed for the freedom and independence I had known prior to my accident. I also hated being a burden to anyone. Mike says it's my Achilles heel, not wanting to appear vulnerable, not wanting to admit that I need help. He's right, and although the circumstances had dictated that I get very good at asking for help over the last few months, at some point, I just got tired of it. I wanted to relearn how to drive.

To say that Mike was apprehensive would be an understatement, and I shared his hesitations. I knew it was not going to be easy and that it certainly involved a fair amount of risk, but I was willing and ready. I was also well aware of the potential problems: my right side had been more damaged by the strokes so using my right foot on the brake and gas pedals would be difficult, my reaction times were slower because it took my brain longer to process information, my spatial awareness and depth perception were not what they used to be, and I had visual cuts in the lower right quadrants of both eyes, so I would have to compensate for that in the car. There were many reasons why driving may not be a good idea, but I wouldn't know until I tried.

The Rehab Institute downtown had a driving program, and thanks to the help of a good friend, I was able to get in quickly. The first step was an assessment in a simulator that tested not only my reaction times, but how easily I could move my foot from the gas to the brake, and how much pressure I could exert with my right foot. I did well enough that the next step was to get behind the wheel of a car with a Rehab Institute instructor. *Whoa!* Driving for the first time was the most overwhelming, frightening experience I have ever had. I struggled with multi-tasking and here I was driving – an activity that requires constant and complex multi-tasking. My brain was on overload, but I was determined. Somehow, I "passed" but barely.

I knew my confidence would grow the more I drove, so I had to do it, even if it was scary. We instructed the kids that if I was driving, there was to be no radio, no questions, virtually no noise at all. I needed complete silence to concentrate. It took all my brainpower at first to keep my eyes focused on the road and my other senses alert. As luck would have it, in the first few weeks, I had my first fender bender. It was on a Sunday morning, and for some reason, Mike had to be at church early, so he drove himself and left before us. I loaded up the family a little later and drove the short distance to Nativity. As I was pulling into a parking space, I accidentally hit the gas instead of the brake and took out an entire iron railing in the parking lot while who knows how many churchgoers looked on. Someone ran inside and told Mike I had an accident. He, of course, panicked and darted to the parking lot. Much to his relief, he quickly discovered that the only casualties involved were the iron railing and my pride.

I was mortified. How embarrassing! And I was upset – it was frightening. The staff at Nativity was so gracious. When we offered to pay to have the railing replaced, the business manager said, "We've been wanting to rip that out for years. You just saved us the trouble!" Mike was not so cavalier about it all. He was worried about leaving me alone while he traveled for work. I had to convince him I was fine. I had let my guard down, so it was a good reminder that I could not let myself get too comfortable behind the wheel.

The independence I gained once I was able to drive was a huge milestone in my recovery. It's also something I will never take for granted. I remember pre-accident how much I complained about having to drive everyone around all the time and griping about the amount of time I spent in the car. After having that taken away from me for a while, I came to appreciate it all the more. I will never complain about driving again! I will never complain about most things again – I am lucky to be alive and have people who love me. All else is minutia.

Ironically, at the same time I was learning to drive, Courtney was also learning to drive. Mike didn't have much time to take her out to practice, and I remember he would come back home so frustrated. "Be patient with her!" I scolded him one afternoon, "Driving is hard!" He looked at me like I was out of my mind. "Seriously," I continued, "there's so much to think about and be aware of. It takes a great deal of concentration. It's really difficult."

Despite the fact that Mike almost laughed out loud, he and I both knew I was right. I also knew that had I not gone through what I had gone through, I would not have this level of understanding and insight into what it felt like to be a new driver. In numerous circumstances, I found that I had empathy for people in different ways than I did before. I knew what it was like to have to learn something new, to struggle, to fail.

This new-found empathy has been yet another blessing in our lives, particularly with our youngest daughter Halley. During the spring before my accident, we had Halley tested because we suspected there might be some learning disabilities present. Following my accident, with the help of Kaitlyn and my dear friend Elizabeth, the diagnostic process was completed and the tests confirmed our suspicions. It was determined that Halley had a variety of learning disabilities, including some social skill impairments that made it difficult for her to read social cues, appropriately filter her own comments, follow along and partici-pate in conversations, and make direct eye contact.

Following my brain injury, I struggled with these exact same things, and I completely understood how Halley must have felt much of the time. When you appear "normal" physically, people just assume you are, in fact, functioning at a normal level. For some reason, it is far more difficult for people to extend you a little bit of grace or civility if you look just like them, but if you have some sort of obvious disability or impairment, people will generally bend over backward to accom-modate you. I realized that I had done that myself in the past, and that even with Halley, I had probably placed unrealistic expectations on her because I didn't understand. Now, I did. I know that I am a far better mother to Halley in the aftermath of my injuries than I was before. I "get" her and am willing to advocate for her in a way that I don't know I could have before. I will do whatever it takes to make sure she gets what she needs in order to learn and thrive, and when her heart gets broken at times because someone doesn't understand her, I am truly there to share her pain and to help her carry on. So much good from such a horrible situation – thank you, God.

Chapter 13

ANSWERED PRAYERS

"Ask and it will be given to you; seek and you will find; knock and the door will be opened to you. For everyone who asks, receives; and the one who seeks, finds; and to the one who knocks, the door will be opened."

MATTHEW 7:7-8

MIKE

We frequently spent time in lengthy conversations with family, friends, and medical professionals about what was "normal" and what was not, and one thing became very clear to me. "Normal" is whatever gifts you're given on that particular day. You can't look at "healing" in its totality ever. You have good days and you have bad days. If it's a good day, you rejoice and give thanks. If it's a bad day, you still rejoice and give thanks and offer it up for the sake of someone else who perhaps needs it more than you. I remember my mom saying that to my siblings and me thousands of times while we were growing up – "offer it up." I didn't fully understand that then, but I sure do now, and I give thanks for the amazing model of faith my mom was for me. She, herself, had survived a devastating head-on collision years before that left her with many physical and mental injuries, so even though she was unable to come out after Terri's accident, she was there with us in spirit, imparting her deep faith-filled wisdom and drawing me back to that incredible foundation she had laid.

We took one day at a time, and when it seemed like more than we could bear, we prayed, and then we moved forward. In November, we said some extra prayers as we headed back to St. Luke's on the Plaza so that Terri could have the first of two stents and coils placed in her carotid arteries. Although she was healing, the arteries, at a certain spot, had been stretched thin, which weakened them. Stents were necessary to fortify the walls of the arteries to keep them open. At the time of Terri's injury, blood had pooled at those stretched sites and created pseudoaneurysms. This meant that as blood continued to flow through the arteries, there was a risk that blood clots could form and go to her brain, which would result in further strokes. They needed to place coils inside each aneurysm to obliterate them. The plan was to place one stent and one coil in November and then wait awhile to make sure that Terri recovered and that everything healed properly. If all went well, the second stent and coil would be placed the following summer. These were risky procedures but necessary.

TERRI

"Necessary" didn't make it any less frightening. The last time a doctor was poking around my carotid arteries, I was teetering on the brink of death. *What if something went wrong with these procedures? What if I still wasn't strong enough to tolerate surgery? What if they got in there and discovered more complications?* I didn't even like going to my follow-up doctors' appointments, but now I had to check in to the hospital and spend the night. Common prootcol for these procedures was to report to the Neuro-ICU, the same unit where I spent those tentative first few days following my middle of the night transport to St. Luke's. Granted, I didn't remember any details of the Neuro-ICU, but the thought of returning there was unsettling for me. I can't even imagine what it must have been like for Mike.

Many of the same nurses were there, and as we walked in, they were utterly shocked to see me functioning so well and maybe even more flabbergasted by how tall I am – they had only seen me lying down! Their warm welcome did little to calm my nerves, and as they prepared me for the procedures, I only grew more anxious. It took three tries to get the IV in my arm, all the while, I couldn't stop shivering, partly because I was freezing and partly because I was totally terrified. Looking around at the masked faces, the bright lights, the cold, sterile machinery, I could hardly believe I was back there again, and all I could wonder to myself was when is this going to be over? When is this entire ordeal *ever* going to be truly over?

Fortunately, the doctors were able to place the first stent and coil without any further complications, and I recovered beautifully, just in time for my family to arrive for Thanksgiving. With Father Ron's approval, it was agreed that my mom would be brought into the Catholic Church that weekend at the Saturday evening Mass. She had continued to meet with Peggy Shrick over the phone after returning to Utah and deeply desired to be baptized at our church because she was so touched by the community there that she had come to experience first-hand during my recovery.

I was so excited to have my family there – all my siblings and their families, my aunt and uncle, and my parents – but prior to everyone's arrival, I had a moment (or two or a thousand) of sheer panic and even dread. It seemed like too much — too overwhelming. I loved to host before my accident, but now, the thought of it was too big for me to wrap my head around. I was used to having everything "just so," and I still wanted it that way, but I was no longer capable of pulling it off like I had been before, so I had to let it go. You'd think I would've been better at that by this point, but it was still so hard. I had to let other people do things for me, and I had to realize and accept that it was not going to be perfect. This Thanksgiving wouldn't earn me a nomination to the Martha Stewart Hall of Fame, but in the end, none of the details I had worried about mattered anyway. Our catered meal was scrumptious, and our paper plate table setting got the job done just as well, if not better, than my expensive china and crystal. What did matter was that we were all together, and this year, we had much for which to be thankful.

I assumed my family had all decided to join us so that they could be there for my mom's big day, and they did, but they also had a sneaky surprise up their sleeves that everyone was in on except for me. On Thanksgiving morning, our five kids announced that they were heading over to the hotel where everyone was staying to have a quick morning cup of coffee. Shortly after they left the house, I started to wish that I had gone with them, so I told Mike I really wanted to go to the hotel too. Mike kept assuring me there was no point — everyone was coming back to our house and would be there soon. He said I should rest, as it was sure to be a long and tiring day ahead. I knew he was right, but throughout the morning, I grew increasingly annoyed. Again, people kept trying to make my decisions for me. I knew what I wanted -- I wanted to join the others at the hotel.

At one point, Mike completely disappeared. I didn't have any idea where he was, so I just assumed he left too. Apparently, I was the only one confined to the limits of the house. My phone rang — it was Mike.

"Come out to the garage" he ordered.

"What?" I questioned, "Where are you?"

"In the garage, come out here."

I could sense the chuckle in his voice. *All right, what in the world is going on?* I opened the door and was greeted by raucous applause and a sea of red. It took me a minute to process what was happening, and then it became beautifully clear. Thanks to my youngest brother David, my entire family was wearing red t-shirts printed with the words, "Give Thanks" and my favorite Scripture verse, Romans 8:28, "We know that all things work for good for those who love God, who are called according to his purpose." It started to click why the kids had left the house and why Mike was so adamant that I stay put. I knew they were all in town for my mom, but I had no idea they had come to celebrate with me. I was overcome with emotion. It was a special moment and a very special day, eclipsed only by my mom's baptism two days later.

I had prayed so long for my mom to become Catholic that the fact it was actually happening almost didn't seem real. When she told me a few months before about her promise to me, I was overwhelmed. Of course, it took me getting hit by a car, but honestly, if I had to do it all over again, I would in a heartbeat. Her joining the Church was just that important to me, and now, here we were. I was going to walk with her down the aisle to the baptismal font in front of our entire congregation. The "walking down the aisle in front of the entire congregation" part was slightly nerve-racking for me. I hoped I didn't trip or fall or in any way embarrass myself or my mom on this occasion. I wanted it to be all about her and the incredibly significant step she was taking in her faith life.

The Mass was packed both with regular parishioners who always attended the Saturday liturgy, but also with numerous non-parishioners who came specifically to support my mom. As I walked with her down the aisle, I caught a glimpse of many faces I recognized, but one in particular, Chris, stood out among all the rest. She was one of my phenomenal nurses from St. Luke's on the Plaza. She was the one who even came in on her day off to check on me and the one who braided my hair and fixed me up for the visits from the kids. Chris was extra special, and my dad was especially attached to her. I saw tears in his eyes as we passed her, and I was once again overwhelmed with thanksgiving. God had placed so many amazing people in our path, people who loved and cared for not just me, but my entire family, exceptionally well. We were blessed, and God just kept heaping the blessings upon us one after the other. Truly, our cup runneth over.

Witnessing my mom's baptism was awesome. This moment was the culmination of many years of prayer, and given the events of the past six months, it felt even more momentous to be standing next to her. Unbeknownst to my mom, as we made our way to the font, Kaitlyn's angelic voice rang out from the choir loft. She sang "Carry Your Candle," by Chris Rice. My mom was completely surprised and totally moved by her granddaughter's beautiful performance of such a beautiful song.

As Mass continued, my mom was also confirmed and received her First Communion. It was a wonderful thing for my entire family to finally be united in one faith and to receive the sacrament of the Eucharist together. I told my mom I was so happy she could share her faith with my dad because as much as my prayer had been about my mom, it was also for my dad's benefit. All those years, he faithfully went to Mass by himself. Now he would have my mom by his side. Later, my dad thanked me. He told me he had never wanted to push my mom, but he wished he had tried harder. He said this was all because of me. Of course, I take no credit — God is good and knows what He's doing. He has a plan and a timetable all His own, and if we didn't believe it before, now we knew for sure that He CAN bring goodness out of suffering. We were living proof.

MIKE

During Kay's baptism, I kept remembering all the mornings I would come downstairs to find Terri sitting on the floor with her back against the cabinet in our living room, deep in prayer or writing in her journal. Without fail, when I would ask what she was praying for, her answer was always the same, "My mom." I was truly watching an answer to prayer unfold before my eyes, and it brought me to my knees. This is why we're here, to live and spread the Gospel of Jesus, and because of Terri, Kay was now baptized into the Body of Christ. It was nothing shy of a miracle, really. God does answer prayers—not always in our time or in our way, but He DOES answer.

Life kept moving forward. The holidays came and went, the kids were busy with school and various activities, and Terri continued to improve. I was traveling quite a bit for work, still trying to help put together the sale of the company, which finally concluded in February. It was a difficult time for me, trying to balance being a good husband and father with being a good leader at work. Selling a company is always a stressful enterprise, and I knew many people would lose their jobs. I wasn't completely sure if I would have a job when it was all said and done.

As it turned out, I *did* have a job, but it was going to be in Milwaukee. I had moved my family before for jobs – five times to be exact – but I could not do it this time. There was no way I could uproot everyone, not after what we had just gone through. Terri was still rehabbing and needed her support system of friends and doctors close by. The kids needed their friends and normal routines now more than ever. Nope, I couldn't do it, and when I told Terri, I reassured her that I would not ask her to pack up and move again. That left us with two choices, either I quit and try to find a new job or I travel to Milwaukee during the week and come home on weekends. We opted for the latter.

My new normal involved flying out usually on Sunday evenings or very early Monday morning and flying back home late Thursday night or early Friday morning. I knew it wasn't a viable long-term solution, but I was willing to make the best of it for the short-term. Two years is what I told Terri I could handle. After that, we would have to re-assess.

The next twenty-four months were brutal. I was undeniably miserable, but as always, God is good and His saving grace for me during this time came in the form of a generous, Christian man — my boss, Dave. Dave and his wife had three daughters, roughly the same ages as three of our girls, and they lovingly welcomed me as a surrogate into their family, even having me for dinner and fellowship every Wednesday night. I loved working with Dave, and if I could have worked with him in Kansas City, I would have stayed in that job forever. He was an oasis for me in a time where I again felt like I was wandering in the desert. We shared many things in common, especially our faith. He even took me on my first and only three-day silent retreat. It was amazing. I don't think I had ever been that quiet for that long. In the silence, God *does* speak, and I needed to hear His voice like never before.

TERRI

Having Mike gone all week was incredibly taxing. I needed him home but I tried never to let him see that. I didn't want him to feel the burden of being needed at home because there was nothing he could do about it. I wanted him to see that I was capable and independent and that I could handle it so he didn't worry. It was hard enough for him to miss so much of the kids' activities and to try to pack a week's worth of family life into one weekend. I knew he was miserable, but there was no opportunity here in Kansas City with the new company. If he wanted to work here, he would have to quit and embark on a time-consuming and risky job search. We agreed that two years was doable, so we put our heads down and plowed ahead.

Time flew by and as that two-year mark approached, I knew something had to give. Traveling was taking its toll on Mike physically, and his absence was not good for our marriage or our family. After the staff of the hotel in Milwaukee where he always stayed sent him a personal, signed Christmas card and I learned that the hotel restaurant had named a breakfast after him, I realized just how much time he spent away from home and I knew we had to devise a different plan.

As we weighed our options, it appeared that moving to Milwaukee was the most logical. Mike loved his job and working alongside Dave, and I was doing considerably better. Kaitlyn was already in college, Courtney would be graduating high school at the end of that school year, John Milton would be graduating eighth grade, and Halley was still young enough that a move would not impact her significantly. That left Abby, who would be right smack dab in the middle of high school. *Ugh.* She was not happy when we discussed the possibility of relocating to Wisconsin during a family meeting. We were ruining her life, and she was devastated. I wasn't necessarily happy about the move myself, but as the clock kept ticking down, we kept finding ourselves without other choices. That is, until Mike was offered a job with Marsh. The offer came exactly two years to the day from the sale of his previous company, the day he was offered the job with Dave in Milwaukee, the day he agreed to take it, but only for two years. God is good – two years came and went and Mike was now employed in Kansas City. It was a tremendous weight lifted off our shoulders not to have to pack up and relocate our family. It felt like maybe, finally, we might be able to return to some version of a slightly altered normal life.

Chapter 14

FORGIVENESS

"Stop judging and you will not be judged. Stop condemning and you will not be condemned. Forgive and you will be forgiven."

LUKE 6:37

MIKE

People always ask, "Did you sue the driver?" I guess in our litigious culture that just seems like the most logical scenario. We *did* hire a lawyer – our friend, Clay, but we did not sue the driver. Clay wasn't opposed to that at first, and he actually advised us to wait and see how much medical care Terri would end up needing. In those early days, the doctors were saying she might need some sort of nursing home facility, perhaps permanently, as she might never regain her full faculties or be able to resume her normal responsibilities. The driver called the hospital right after the accident to inquire about Terri. At that point, he was told she was doing fine, but as she began to decline, Clay advised us not to have any further direct contact with him.

As it became clear that Terri was going to not only survive, but exceed the doctors' expectations in terms of recovery time, it also became clear that legally, we had no case. The police investigation was not able to assign significant blame to the driver who hit Terri, or to anyone for that matter. According to the police report, he was swerving to avoid hitting another car. There was no alcohol or drugs involved in any way. It was what it was, simply an accident, or as the State of Kansas referred to it, a "no fault" accident. Even if there had been legal grounds for a suit, I honestly don't know that we would have pursued it. That's not really our style. The only reason we might've considered it would have been if Terri was truly incapacitated and we needed a settlement to cover expenses.

After discussing it at length with Clay, we decided we didn't want to go to court. We didn't have a good chance of winning anyway, and it would've meant putting Terri through the trauma of reliving that day over and over again. What we *did* want was to meet the driver face to face. We felt strongly that in order for there to be some degree of closure to this situation, we needed to seek reconciliation, and personally, I wanted answers. From the onset, I had struggled to understand exactly what had happened and how Terri ended up in the middle of the street in oncoming traffic. One of the police officers asked me if it was possible that Terri ran out in front of the car on purpose. I knew that nothing could be farther from the truth, but the fact that the truth was unknown tugged at me – I needed to know.

Initially, the desire for forgiveness was for US. It was something we felt we needed to do for our own benefit. I can't say I had any strong feelings of animosity toward this man, but I didn't *want* to ever harbor any anger or resentment toward him, and I often wondered how *he* felt about us, the accident, everything. The last time he saw Terri was at the scene of the accident. I couldn't imagine what he thought or felt at that moment or since. I also just wondered who he was, what he looked like, what he did for a living, what his story was. I thought that if we could meet, maybe all of us could start to put the whole thing behind us once and for all.

TERRI

I wished I could remember exactly how it all happened so that I could give Mike the clarity he so desperately longed for, but honestly, part of me was so thankful I couldn't remember. Not only could I not remember the actual accident, but I couldn't remember anything from the day of. I couldn't even recall much of anything from several months before the accident. The doctors explained that it takes time for our brains to transfer information from short-term memory to long-term, so anything that was "in process" from short-term to long-term in my brain was totally lost. At one point, Mike had suggested that maybe we should move because we had to drive past the scene of the accident every single time we entered or exited our sub-division. He was afraid it was too traumatic for me. I am sure it gave him pause as he drove past it daily, but I was honestly unmoved by it because there was absolutely zero memory of it.

I understood Mike's need for answers, but I wasn't too concerned with that. I *did* want to meet the driver. I wanted to be able to tell him I forgave him. I kept thinking about how I would feel if I were him, if I had hit someone. I would want to apologize and I would want to be forgiven. I never really felt angry at him. I was angry that my life was forever altered, but my anger was directed more at the situation and less toward him. I didn't even know him. How could I be angry with him?

MIKE

Our lawyer thought a face-to-face meeting was a bad idea, and apparently so did his, but despite the opposition of both lawyers' legal counsel, we pushed for it anyway. After extensive back and forth negotiations, the terms of the meeting were finally set, and we agreed to a neutral site, the library at the Olathe, KS Courthouse on September 29, 2009. This was the feast of the Archangels: Michael, Gabriel, and Raphael. We took that as a good sign. Both lawyers would be present, and we would have one hour.

Terri and I arrived early, nervous with anticipation. *What was this guy going to be like?* I was a little worried about how Terri was going to handle this meeting. I imagined it would be far more difficult for her than for me. She was living with the aftermath of the driver's actions and would forever be reminded of that day. I also hoped her filter was "on" more for her own sake than for mine. We went for a coffee since we had time to spare and we prayed, prayed that the Holy Spirit would be present in the room and that our hearts would be open and gracious.

We entered the library first and were met by both lawyers for a brief "prep" before the driver was brought in. As soon as he stepped across the threshold, I felt the Holy Spirit right there. There were absolutely no bad vibes in the space, no evil intentions, just the presence of God and the archangel Michael surrounding us with a hedge of protection against any temptation toward anger or hatred. We stood and walked toward the good-looking thirty-five-year-old with hands outstretched. He was a man, just like me, and as it turned out, a father also, just like me.

TERRI

I asked if I could open with a prayer, and our lawyers acquiesced. I don't remember exactly what I said, something about forgiveness and mercy and God's plan. I was too emotional to make it all the way through it with any sort of eloquence. I had been fearful to see him, to actually see him and look him in the eye, and now here we were, sitting at the same table in the same room. Before my prayer was even finished, I knew there was nothing to fear here. He was a human being, a humble man, and I was sure we had made the right decision by asking to meet.

The first thing he asked me was, "How are you?" He explained that he had tried to find out and that he thought I was all right at first. Once he was unable to get updates, he became worried and the not knowing had loomed over him ever since. Mike explained in full detail what I had gone through. The driver and I both cried as Mike told him about the night at St. Luke's when I almost didn't make it and about the year and a half of recovery since.

As part of the negotiation process, we had agreed to sign numerous legal documents releasing the driver from any culpability, regardless of what was said in this meeting. In other words, if he admitted to being on his phone or speeding or something like that, we agreed that we would not pursue any further legal action. He did not admit to being on his phone or to speeding or to any behaviors that would have contributed to the accident. What he did say was, "I'm sorry." This struck me because he was truly free in this meeting to say it, and probably had not felt free in the last year and half to say those words aloud. I heard the words, listened to them, let them soak in, and thanked him for saying them.

It also struck me when he revealed that he relives the accident every single day in his mind. *What torture that must be!* I was left with physical injuries, some wounds that had healed over time and still some that would never heal, but I was so blessed to not have to repeatedly relive the trauma in my mind. He was physically unscathed, but left with the permanent memory, an emotional wound that is not easily erased or healed. My heart went out to him.

MIKE

During our conversation, he tried to provide as many details as he could. It all happened so fast that it was difficult for him to recount much more than what we already knew. After hitting Terri, his car spun around and hit a brick wall, and eventually, luckily, landed in the grass. The results could have been far more devastating.

As our one-hour limit approached, one of the lawyers asked if there was anything else that needed to be said. The driver explained that at the time of the accident his wife was six months pregnant. He said that since the accident, even after his son was born, it was impossible for him to be truly happy or to enjoy being a father because he could not stop worrying about Terri. He did not know the extent of her injuries, so seeing her was bittersweet. He was glad she was alive, but he could see that she had suffered due to his actions. We immediately assured him that we felt total and complete forgiveness toward him, and at those words, you could literally see the weight lifted from his shoulders. And at that same moment, the whole ordeal felt wiped clean for me. Questions answered. Door closed. You can't see the face of Christ if you hold on to anger, and from that point forward, I have never again felt anything but peace about the entire situation. Our meeting ended in a hug, and that was it. We have never heard from or seen him again, and don't need to. I can't even remember now what he looks like or what his name is, and in all honesty, it doesn't even matter.

KAITLYN

I never thought too terribly much about the driver who hit my mom. I may have felt some anger at first, but it was what it was, just an accident. He didn't mean to hit her, and I'm sure she didn't mean to run out in front of him. Although I didn't have any strong desire or need to ever meet him, I think it was very brave and extremely healthy that my mom and dad did. It provided some degree of closure for them, and I imagine it did the same for him as well.

ABBY

While my mom was in the hospital, my sole focus was on her. Trying to process what was happening and wondering whether she was going to get better was enough to occupy my thoughts 24/7. As she began to heal and things settled down a little, I *did* start to think about the driver. After I read the accident report, it was obvious that it was just that — an accident. It was no one's fault. That is a dangerous street, and what happened was completely unforeseen, unpredictable, and unavoidable. Blaming the driver is just a waste of time and energy. If anything, I feel compassion toward him. I know that when I make a mistake, even a small one, I tend to fixate on it and end up feeling awful about it way longer than I probably should. I am much harder on myself than anyone else ever could be on me. I cannot begin to fathom how he must've felt and maybe even still feels to this day. I truly hope he feels forgiven and that he has let himself off the hook. We've moved on. Hopefully he has too.

Chapter 15

LESSONS IN LIFE, LOVE AND FAITH

"No, in all these things we conquer overwhelmingly through him who loved us. For I am convinced that neither death, nor life, nor angels, nor principalities, nor present things, nor future things, nor powers, nor height, nor depth, nor any other creature will be able to separate us from the love of God in Christ Jesus our Lord."

ROMANS 8:37-39

HALLEY

I was so young at the time of my mom's accident that I honestly don't remember in any great detail what she was like before. I *do* remember, after she came home, the moment I knew she was "back." It was my first soccer game she came to after everything had happened. I was not playing very well, but I heard her yelling from the sidelines, "Go Halley! Go Halley!" Hearing her voice stopped me in my tracks. I hadn't heard her cheering me on for a while, and I realized how much I missed that and needed it.

I have never forgotten that moment, and now, almost ten years later, I can see the symbolism in it. There she was on the sidelines of the soccer field, supporting and encouraging me when I needed it most, just like she does every single day of my life. Thinking your mom is going to die when you're six is a lot to handle. When I heard her voice that day, I knew she wasn't going to die, at least not anytime soon. I knew she was going to be in my life for a long time. It was such a relief! As I grow up, I think about her on the sidelines of my life, and it brings me great happiness to know that she'll be there for all of it — graduations, wedding, grandchildren.

Thinking about my mom's accident still gets to me. I know we could have lost her, and when I think about what life would have been like without her, I cannot imagine how we could've survived. God knew how much we needed her. Today, my mom is my hero! I can see the face of God in her smile. She is my role model of faith and determination. This tragedy brought our family closer, and it taught me to live every day as if it could be your last because you never know. My advice to anyone going through a difficult time is to never give up. God does have a plan for us — sometimes it's hard to see what that is, but if we keep the faith, He will reveal it in time, and when we look back, we will be able to see all the good He brought from it. I love my family and feel so blessed to be Terri and Mike Kern's daughter.

JOHN MILTON

The accident feels like a lifetime ago, but I can still see the effects today. It was so significant that I don't believe we will ever fully move on from it. The only thing we can do at this point is to try and live the new life that has been placed in front of us. My mom clearly affected so many people – even before the accident. It was evident from the outpouring of support just how many people loved her, and I was moved by that. I was so thankful for that and for our family and all the ways everyone came together during that difficult time. I never doubted that we were going to be well cared for and that in the end, everything would be all right, no matter how it all turned out.

I did not, however, credit this to God. I still don't. This tragedy shattered my faith rather than strengthened it. I just can't get on board with God if He would allow something like this to happen. I can't understand it. People have tried to explain it in ways that they think will help, but it hasn't. I admire my parents' rock solid faith. I just have a difficult time agreeing with it. Maybe that will change someday, but for now, we respectfully agree to disagree, and when I'm home, I go to Mass with them and pray at meals and do all the things they expect of me. I owe them that, and I am grateful for the patience and unconditional love they show me every single day.

ABBY

Nothing in our lives ever went back to the way it was before the accident. As time wore on, I actually started to forget what my mom was like prior to the accident as I slowly began to adjust to the new normal that was replacing all that had been. Her recovery has been remarkable to watch, but as much as I'd like to forget that it ever happened, the accident left behind permanent reminders that will never go away. My mom can no longer multi-task and she isn't able to control her emotions as easily as she did before. Sometimes it's humorous when she starts to laugh uncontrollably when she wins at a card game, but other times it's painful to watch as she bursts into tears over something small and insignificant. It is difficult to see her defeated by some of her physical limitations from the accident. Since she can't see out of her right side and has balance issues, she falls easily. This breaks my heart because I can see how disappointed and frustrated she becomes.

Despite her struggles, my mom is and continues to be an inspiration to the hundreds of people who walked this journey with us. She is THE strongest woman I know with a love for Jesus that is indescribable and unshakable. She has taught us all what it means to come through adversity with a new-found strength and faith.

As for me, I am more guarded now than I was before. I tend to expect the worst because I never want to be surprised again like I was that night we thought we were losing my mom. Eventually, I resolved the anger I felt toward my father. I realized what he was going through, and I began to understand the heavy burden he carried during that time. I know he did the absolute best he could, and that's all any of us can do at any given time.

My parents' faith is so strong. I struggle a little. There is no doubt in my mind that when science fails, a higher power takes over. I witnessed that first hand, and I believe it whole-heartedly. I also believe in the power of prayer. Maybe it didn't "save" my mom in the sense that she didn't return to her pre-accident self, but it certainly saved us, and I know it helps my mom every day to cope with her life as it is now and to embrace the cross she has been given. I often wonder why my mom survived when someone else in a similar situation may not have made it. I don't know the answer to that question, but pondering it has given me a different perspective on life and its meaning.

I'm in nursing school now, and I credit this journey with sparking that desire within me. I watched the nurses take such incredible care of my mom. They were compassionate for the whole person and went above and beyond to be attentive to our needs as well. They were a source of light during those dark days early on, and they inspired me with their care-taking ministry. I hope and pray that I can emulate their example.

COURTNEY

It was strange to hear people call my mom a miracle because I know how determined she is. For me, it was a given that she would fight continuously to get her life back. I couldn't have predicted how well she would do or how many expectations she would surpass, but I never doubted that she *would* overcome all the obstacles in her way. She's not the same, that's for sure, but over time, I think she has adapted to her new self, and we have too.

I no longer see my mom as invincible, which has been a good thing. I still look up to her and admire her, but I see her as a human being now, which means I can relate to her on a whole new and better level. I actually used to be intimidated by how athletic my mom was. I'm not much of an athlete so I usually turned her down when she asked me to run with her before the accident. Although I know she now mourns the loss of her ability to run, I'll jump at the chance to go on a nice walk with her any day.

I feel honored to be there for her now, whereas before I assumed she never needed help. Since the accident, she can no longer multi task in the same way she used to, but I like being clued in on her many lists and errands now. It's more of a partnership.

I see in my mother now the beautiful virtue of humility every single day, the kind of humility that allows your kids and husband to be part of your healing process. She could have shut us out and kept us in the dark, but instead, she graciously let us be a part of her journey, and that has been the healthiest thing for me. I feel changed in that I try to never take my family for granted, and very deeply mourn for people when they lose parents because it could have so easily been me.

KAITLYN

It was a mistake to act like everything was all right when it wasn't. I knew, even as it was all happening, that I needed more time to let it soak in. I didn't get that time, so I stuffed everything I was feeling deep down and moved forward because that was what I was supposed to do. Consequently, I harbored a great deal of anger toward my dad, resentment at having to grow up too fast, unresolved grief at the loss of our former lives, and fear of losing my mom again. Once I left home and headed off to college, those suppressed emotions started to surface, and I struggled for a little while as I tried to work through it all.

I've come a long way but readily admit that I am still very much a work in progress. My dad and I are working to rebuild our relationship, and as I grow further into adulthood, I am starting to better understand who he is and to see just how similar we are. I am far more open in terms of accepting others and empathizing with what they've gone through and why they act the way they do. We all have a story. I've learned to focus on what's really important and to be thankful for my family and friends.

For a long time, I wanted nothing to do with my faith. My mom's accident, coupled with my subsequent struggles to cope with it, all but destroyed what was left of my faith, but lately I have found myself searching. I am just not sure what I should believe to embrace fully the Catholic faith, or any faith for that matter. I wish I had the faith my parents do. I recognize that it helps them find beauty and it brings them comfort. I want that – who doesn't? I'm open though, and I am so grateful every day for the family I was born in to and for the life I have been given.

COLEEN

It's so easy to think we know people. If you would've asked me in 2008, I would've said, "I know Terri." We had known each other from church for three to four years prior to her accident. We were friends. Our children were friends. That's why it was so shocking for me to find out how little I really knew about my friend Terri in the aftermath of her accident.

I'll never forget when I found out she was hit. I had actually heard the accident reported on the radio while in my kitchen on that brisk, beautiful spring day. I didn't know it was Terri, of course, until later. When I found out she was struck while on a run, I couldn't believe it. *Terri was a runner?* I had no idea! How could I have spent time with her and not known how much she loved to run?

Then, there were the incredible numbers of people who also "knew" Terri who came swarming from every direction to help in any way they could. *Who were all these people?* They were from so many different places — not just from our church family or neighborhood, but from other churches, other neighborhoods, other walks of life. I quickly realized that what I knew of Terri and her life was only one "sliver" of a much bigger pie. All of us were just one sliver, one piece, and as we came together, we created this beautiful mosaic of faces and places and lives, all of which were touched by Terri Kern. It made me keenly aware of how easily we claim to *know* our friends and neighbors…. but do we really? And what does it even mean to say we *know* someone? It also made me keenly aware of how we move throughout our lives, often having no idea who we're impacting.

There's no doubt that Terri impacted me in ways so profound I am still discovering them after all this time. When we moved the furniture out of Mike and Terri's front room to make the "in-law suite" for Kay and Allan, I saw the cabinet that Terri always sat against in the mornings when she started her days in prayer. I had heard about Terri's daily prayer life, but seeing the way the finish was literally worn away on that cabinet from the countless hours she sat there in prayer, I was blown away. The image of that affected me deeply. It was a testimony to her persistence and faithfulness. MY friend was a prayer warrior! A giant!

I kept telling people when Terri's life hung in the balance that God was not going to take her. I knew then, and I am even more sure of it now, that Terri is one of God's soldiers, one of His finest. Right after her accident, I had a vision. I did not yet know any of the details of the accident, where exactly she was hit or where she landed, but my vision was of an angel – a white, gossamer gust of wind. The angel deftly picked Terri up off the pavement, carefully cradled her in its arms, and gingerly laid her in a patch of grass. Imagine my surprise when I found out that she did indeed land in a patch of grass. There's no doubt that God has work for her to do, work still undone and yet to be revealed.

Just to be clear, I was not the kind of person who "had" visions. That was new for me, but I attribute it to Terri and the way her example of faith was slowly transforming me. Terri inspired me to start a focused regimen of daily prayer, a practice that has drawn me deeper into my relationship with God than I ever thought possible. It has drawn me deeper into an awareness and understanding of the angels, too. They're real – there's no question in my mind. Interestingly enough, several months after Terri's accident, she and Mike hosted a dinner to say thank you to the many people who supported their family during their time of need. Terri gave Lynn, Elizabeth, and me small angel figurines. Mine still sits in my prayer room and reminds me that there are no coincidences.

In the last few years, Terri and I grew apart. My family moved north of the city, more than an hour's drive, our kids grew up, and over time, it became harder and harder to get together with friends from the old neighborhood. It is no coincidence that Terri and I reconnected as this book was bring written. I had never shared with her how profoundly she had changed my life. I am so blessed to be able to tell her that now and to have the opportunity to rekindle a friendship that I believe was God ordained from the beginning. Terri is an integral part of *my* mosaic, a piece of my life and faith story that cannot be erased. I can only imagine how many other people can say the same about this amazingly strong woman of faith.

DR. PAUL CAMARATA

After seeing the bilateral strokes and Terri's extreme clinical condition when she arrived at St. Luke's, I never would have imagined she would recover to the extent she has. That is why I painted such a potentially bleak recovery picture for Mike. As we elevated her blood pressure, it created additional problems, which necessitated further blood transfusions, but it provided badly needed perfusion to her brain until the arterial dissections could heal.

I know that Terri spent many long months in recovery and rehabilitation, but witnessing her recovery, given the strokes I remember seeing on her MRI scans, is difficult to explain by natural means alone. I often pray to God and for miraculous intercession by saints for my patients, and I have no doubt that Terri's recovery was nothing short of a miracle.

MIKE

"In sickness and in health..." How many people say those words without realizing the profound commitment and sacrifice they imply? I am sure I had no idea when I first uttered those words to Terri how far or deep our marriage vows would take us. God is good, and in His infinite wisdom, he allowed me my own season of suffering prior to Terri's accident so that I could first receive what I then had to give. It was prophetic. The perspective I gained during that time allowed me to be a much more compassionate and patient caregiver to my wife than I would have been otherwise. Terri and I have each known what it means to truly rely on one another, and after having done that, it makes all the small stuff we might've worried about or argued about before seem far less important.

I discovered that suffering can and does give birth to great joy. We may not necessarily always recognize or embrace the joy right at the moment of suffering, but if we trust and we are patient, God always reveals His divine plan and always delivers us right into the arms of joy greater than any pain we have endured. We experienced that time and again throughout this journey. If you don't agree with that statement or believe my testimony, I would simply offer Jesus, Mary, and Joseph as witnesses to the profound joy that they received through unbelievable suffering on this earth. You could also look at the apostles, or if you need examples closer to our time – Pope St. John Paul II or St. Mother Theresa. All, and I mean all, encountered profound suffering prior to their human deaths.

I define "joy" as clarity around the "who," "what," "when," "where," and "how" I am supposed to serve and interact with others in this world. Notice I did not include "why." In my experience, questioning the "why" often distorts my clarity. The "why" is often filled with smoke and mirrors, rabbit holes and dead ends that do nothing to increase my joy.

Who am I to try to answer the question of "why" anyway? I can sometimes see glimpses of meaning and reasoning behind things – there was an awful lot of good that came out of Terri's accident, and I can certainly point to those things and say, "Yes, that is *WHY* this happened," but I would be wrong, or at best, only partially right. In my smallness and limited eternal vision, how can I even begin to ascertain the "why" in the great big scheme of the universe? It's arrogant to try, and that is what I learned. God is good all the time, and all I ever have to do is trust Him.

Another discovery for me was that faith, very simply, is the fuel that allowed me to move from one point to the next and to make life and death decisions with some sense of peace. I have been told to never speak in absolutes, but I can say with great confidence that I would never have had the faith to endure this season of suffering if I did not pray and give thanks every single day. The more I prayed, the more my faith increased. Every time I asked, God showered me with more fuel to keep me going, and every time I thought I couldn't go on, He filled me with more fuel and kept showing me His loving presence made manifest in the many caring people He placed on our path.

On a practical level, I learned that people are much stronger than they give themselves credit. If you asked me prior to 2008 if we would come through this intact as a close family, I might have had some hesitation. I see our family in the same light as the larger community -- if given the chance, they will come through suffering with joy, just as we did.

Finally, communication is key, and in certain areas of our story, it was stellar – the use of journaling and Caring Bridge was incredibly useful for all involved. I made the monumental error of thinking all my children were the exact same, and so I communicated with them as one person. As evidenced by their reflections in this book, they all interpreted the experience differently. I should have spent more time one on one answering questions or simply listening to their concerns and fears. I abdicated my role as a father, which is never acceptable no matter what the situation. I will continue to apologize for my error in judgment for as long as it takes. Eight, almost nine, years later, we are still discussing and seeking counseling to process the wounds this experience created, and in its own way, that is also bringing about great joy. It is drawing me closer to my children and deeper into an understanding of their hearts and minds. It's allowing me to be the father I was called to be and to get to know my children as adults on a whole new level.

TERRI

Our family references everything as "pre-accident" or "post-accident." April 28, 2008, *is* the day against which all other days are measured and will be forever. It was a defining moment in every possible way, and as I look back, I see innumerable lessons and blessings.

I took so many things for granted before my accident, my faith not the least among them. My plate was full as a wife, mother of five, and active volunteer. With so much busy-ness and so many distractions, it was often difficult to pray and have a relationship with God. I worked at it, I did pray, and I certainly considered myself a person of faith, but once everything was taken from me.... EVERYTHING, but GOD, my choice became simple -- I needed my faith. I cannot even begin to fathom how I could have navigated this experience without my faith, and I know that the faith I had prior to the accident was crucial in preparing me for this season of suffering.

I'm not going to say I never felt angry at God. I definitely felt angry and frustrated at the situation, and sometimes, yes, even a little angry with God. What I realized is that I have a relationship with God, and like any relationship, it ebbs and flows and goes through good times and bad. Just as I can get angry with Mike without the fear of our marriage completely falling apart, I know I can get angry with God without the fear of losing Him. He's big enough to take on my anger and He's certainly big enough to carry my cross. In the throes of my deepest suffering, I clung to Him, and Him alone. I learned that God is truly the only constant in my life, the single un-changing, unwavering, sole source of life and joy that can never be taken away. Once all else was stripped from my life, I saw this with immense clarity, and I understood that no other relationship in my life was as rock solid dependable as my relationship with God.

I didn't always want to pray or feel like praying, especially early in my recovery because it was just too hard. I believe though that we are called to obedience, and that we pray because God asks us to. How I feel about it on any given day is utterly irrelevant. I pray anyway, and the more I pray when I don't want to, the more my desire to pray grows.

Before the accident, my relationship with God was on my terms—now, it is on His.

Relationships are all that matter. I had always been "good" at relationships and friendships, but much like my relationship with God, it had been on my terms. After my accident, I learned how to be truly present to the people I love when *they* need me, not just when I want to make time. Second only to my relationship with God is my relationship with Mike. The decision to marry him is the best decision I have ever made. He fought for me and never gave up. I admire his strength, determination, and perseverance, but most of all, I love his faith. I know that no matter what life throws at us, we can handle it, as long as we are together and we put God first.

There is a phrase I used to repeat over and over, as if I needed convincing, "Do not let your circumstances dictate your joy." Many people confuse joy for happiness. These hold different meanings for me. Happiness is related to one's situation, event, or status in life, etc. Joy is a virtue, a gift and is not dependent on anything external, but rather it radiates from inside. That joy can't be taken away by anyone or anything because it comes from God. I learned how to be joyful despite my circumstances, and I grew closer to Christ in my suffering.

Suffering is going to find us, no matter what. I had always told my children that. It's just part of life. We can choose how to accept it and walk through it. Mike and I were mindful that people were watching to see how we handled this, and we felt a responsibility to witness by our words and actions, so we chose to walk this road with joy.

I also learned the virtue of humility. I was always the one bringing meals to others or helping with carpool, etc. I cannot begin to thank the countless people who prayed for me and my family, took carpool duty, filled in for me on committees., managed my calendar, took the kids to their practices and games, drove me to and from rehab, the list goes on and on. It was and is very overwhelming and humbling to graciously accept the help of others. I finally learned to just smile and say "thank you" because that's all I could say and that's all that needed to be said.

God validated for me the power of persistent prayer when I witnessed my mom's baptism. It was truly the answer to so many years of prayer. Saint Monica had always been, and continues to be, my model of relentless prayer. She prayed for the conversion of her son, Augustine, for over seventeen years without ceasing or losing hope. Her example has inspired me to not give up or give in when my prayers seem to go unheard. Since my accident, I have followed her footsteps as a mother who prays constantly for her children. Life has continued to move on and it hasn't always been easy — I know my children have struggled in the aftermath of my accident, and I worry about them.... a lot. Consequently, I pray for them...a lot. It pains me to realize how my children have struggled as a direct result of this accident. As a mother, I feel somewhat responsible. I was so focused on rehab and recovery that I wasn't in-tune with what my children were going through or the profound impact this had on their lives. I regret this deeply and apologize to each of them. I wanted to be that same mother to them, but I was not, and I still am not. I am different. I am grateful that Mike and all my children accept me for the person I am now. God wills the best for them, I know this.... I WILL continue in persistent prayer for my family.

Because Abby chose the name "Monica" for her Confirmation name, her sponsor, my dear friend Coleen, gave her a St. Monica medal. At a point when I was particularly concerned about one of our children, I asked Abby if I could wear it. It gave me a sense of comfort to unite my prayers with those of a spiritual giant like Monica. If she had the strength and patience to persevere for her son, I know I can hang in there. Her son ended up being one of the greatest saints in the Church.

I don't need my children to be perfect. I'll settle for happy, healthy, faith-filled men and women.

The best prayer is a well-lived life. When my children look back on my life, they won't remember fame or notoriety. Rather, I hope they remember a person who loves being their mother, who fought to come back to them, and is still fighting. I hope when they think of me, they see a woman of faith who did the best she could to love and serve the Lord and to put others' needs ahead of her own. I hope they see God's hand evident in our story, and I pray that by sharing our story, my children can have the gift of closure and peace necessary to move forward.

Suffering can draw us closer to God or drive us further away. It can be a lonely, bitter road to traverse. I know I didn't always walk it with the grace, humility, and patience I should have, but I never gave up. I hope that if anyone reads our story who is in the throes of suffering, they will find comfort in knowing they are not alone and that they will find solace in the arms of God.

Without God, this story would not be what it is. There would've been mountains to move, but no way to budge them. It is by the sheer grace of God that I survived, that I had the will to fight, that I had the faith to keep going, and that we were surrounded by so many loving and supportive people. Any mountains moved were not because of anything we did – it's all on Him. If I have learned anything, it is that there will be more mountains ahead, but I can walk confidently toward them because I know that God is bigger and more powerful than any obstacle in my way. I am living proof that with Him, all things ARE possible, and in the end, He DOES work all things for good.

ACKNOWLEDGEMENTS

We would like to thank our neighbors, friends, the Church of the Nativity Parish community, and the many doctors, nurses, and therapists who helped in Terri's recovery. We continue to be humbled by the countless prayers and acts of charity offered to and for our family.

We would like to especially thank our extended families who put their lives on hold and traveled from Utah, Idaho, Arizona, Kentucky, Oregon, and Washington to minister to us during this most difficult period in our lives.

We are forever grateful to all those who helped make this book a reality. Thank you to our friends and family for their willingness to share their perspectives in writing and in interviews, both face-to face and over the phone. Thank you for sharing your memories, especially the painful ones. Your numerous contributions made this book possible.

A special thank you to our friends who rallied as the book neared completion to assist with final edits. Your keen eye for detail is much appreciated.

Finally, we would like to thank God, the Father, for giving us unfailing strength to walk through this journey.

ABOUT THE AUTHORS

Terri and Mike Kern have been happily married for over twenty-eight years. Together, they have been blessed with five children.

Terri Kern holds a master's degree in social work and splits her time between her family and a number of volunteer organizations.

Mike Kern has a business degree and has worked in insurance brokerage for the past thirty years.

Terri and Mike live in Leawood, Kansas.

This book was written with the assistance of Tina Wendling.

45083954R00105

Made in the USA
San Bernardino, CA
31 January 2017